Building Positive Momentum for Positive Behavior in Young Children

Building Positive Momentum for Positive Behavior in Young Children

STRATEGIES FOR SUCCESS IN SCHOOL AND BEYOND

LISA ROGERS

Jessica Kingsley *Publishers*
London and Philadelphia

First published in 2018
by Jessica Kingsley Publishers
73 Collier Street
London N1 9BE, UK
and
400 Market Street, Suite 400
Philadelphia, PA 19106, USA

www.jkp.com

Library of Congress Cataloging in Publication Data
A CIP catalog record for this book is available from the Library of Congress

British Library Cataloguing in Publication Data
A CIP catalogue record for this book is available from the British Library

ISBN 978 1 78592 774 4
eISBN 978 1 78450 679 7

Printed and bound in Great Britain

FSC
www.fsc.org

MIX
Paper from
responsible sources
FSC® C013056

The accompanying PDF can be downloaded from
www.jkp.com/voucher using the code **FKR2AMm2**

For Orion

My Best Hope for a Beautiful Tomorrow

Teaching and supporting positive behavior is most effective when incorporated throughout the day as a natural part of the routine. Shifting from a reactive response to a preventive focus is an investment of time up front that results in more positive behaviors and less time dealing with problem behaviors.

Students learn appropriate behavior in the same way a child who doesn't know how to read learns to read—through instruction, practice, feedback, and encouragement.

CONTENTS

Dear Teacher,

I love being in your class because we have so much fun and you are so very nice to all of us. I know that sometimes I have a hard time sitting at circle time, but I am so excited and my body shows that by wiggling and moving and bouncing about.

I am trying.

I know that sometimes I have a hard time listening to what you say. There are so many wonderful things happening and I don't want to miss any of it. I look around and pay attention to lots of things and so I miss some of them too.

I am trying.

I know that sometimes I blurt out my ideas without raising my hand. My head is filled with so many ideas and sometimes they come pouring out at the wrong times.

I am trying.

Please know that I am watching you to learn how to be a good, kind and helpful person. Thank you for being patient and kind with me.

I am trying.

A Future Fireman, Nurse, Teacher, Architect, Doctor, Ballerina...

I'm not sure yet.

Chapter 1

INTRODUCTION

PRIMING

Priming is a method of preparing a student for an activity that they will be expected to complete by allowing the student to preview the activity before it is presented for completion.

Priming helps to:

- accommodate the student's preference for predictability

- promote the student's success with the activity

- reduce the likelihood that the student will experience anxiety and stress about what lies ahead (with anxiety and stress at a minimum, the student can *focus his or her efforts on successfully completing activities*).

The following are but a few examples of how priming may be accomplished in a learning setting:

1. Complete a KWL graphic organizer (Know—Want to Know—Learned).

2. Conduct a "picture walk" prior to reading a book/story.

3. Review guiding questions prior to reading a book/story.

4. Practice visualization of upcoming information.

5. Preview a list of activities in a task.

6. Preview key vocabulary terms.

7. Practice with new instructional materials.

8. Discuss what a finished product may include.

9. View multiple work samples that show different styles or ideas.

10. Listen to related music.

11. Experience a prop box or related real objects.

A prop box is a collection of items that represent key ideas throughout the story. By exploring these items prior to reading the story, learners are connected to the content in concrete ways. Meaning, motivation, and successful engagement may be enhanced. When children feel successful in their learning, they are more likely to have confidence as they develop other areas of their cognitive and social-emotional growth.

Adults can use priming to address behavioral skills and development as well. By clarifying what expected behaviors are prior to engaging in a social situation, the child is better prepared to demonstrate those desired behaviors. A visual as in Figure 1.1 may provide clear choices about how to interact with other children. Notice that only desired choices are presented with no mention of problem behaviors.

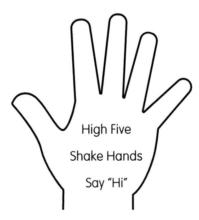

High Five

Shake Hands

Say "Hi"

Figure 1.1 Being a Good Friend

The relationship between adults and children is at the heart of any instructional or behavioral program. This emotional connection creates a strong foundation for instructional, social, and behavioral growth.

APPLIED BEHAVIORAL ANALYSIS

Upon embarking on a scientific and humane approach to building positive momentum toward positive behaviors, a review of the fundamental components of applied behavioral analysis is essential, as outlined in Table 1.1.

Table 1.1 Applied Behavioral Analysis

Antecedent	Behavior	Consequence
The events, action(s), or circumstances that occur immediately before a behavior.	The behavior in objective and specific terms (frequency, intensity and duration).	The action(s) or response(s) that immediately follows the behavior.
To understand and teach positive behaviors, it's essential to analyze the antecedents to problem behaviors. When we understand the antecedents of a behavior, we have better understanding of the contributing factors and possible functions. Rearranging the antecedents can serve to *prevent* the challenging behavior and promote positive behaviors.	The specific behavior that you are focusing on. Typically, this behavior is a problem because it may be distracting, harmful, or detrimental to the well-being of the individual or others. It is important to state the behavior objectively, without emotion, and with specificity so as to clearly understand the situation and to monitor progress accurately.	The term "consequence" is most commonly related to punishment. However, there is another type of consequence and it is instructive in that it serves to teach a more positive behavior. With this understanding of the broader definition of "consequence," problem solving and role playing can be consequences... *instructive consequences.*

Antecedents

Often, the first thought when dealing with challenging or disruptive behavior may be "How do I stop that behavior?" Unfortunately, it is usually quite a bit more complex than that. In trying to change a behavior, it is most imperative to try to understand why that behavior is occurring. Behavior does not occur in a vacuum and may derive from multiple sources of motivation. The child that screams may feel as though no one understands what they are saying. Or they might scream out of an overwhelming need to gain control over a situation. Or they might scream out of pure frustration with themselves or others. Data that includes specific information about what happened immediately prior to the behavior will help to determine the most likely causes. Data on the antecedents should include the date, the time of day, persons involved, the location and the activity the child was doing right before the behavior occurred.

The most common functions of behavior include the following:

- to gain attention from peers and/or adults

- to gain something tangible

- to gain power or control

- to meet a sensory need

- to communicate feelings, wants, and needs

- as a result of a lack of understanding

- to escape or avoid something.

To complicate matters even further, Miltenberger (2008) has outlined that a behavior can serve more than one function. For example, a child might throw objects during class to get out of having to complete academic tasks and then also throw objects on the playground to get attention from the teachers or other students. In this example, the same behavior—throwing objects— serves two different functions depending on the situation and environment surrounding the child.

Once the reasons behind the behavior are better understood, then teachers and parents can provide the most strategic and effective strategy for prevention of that behavior. Prevention can take the form of teaching the desired behavior, self-regulation strategies, or alternative choices for more positive behaviors. Additionally, removing certain stressors may increase the likelihood that the child can demonstrate more positive behaviors. We all act and react differently when under stress, usually for the worse. Even the most competent adult might be less kind and forgiving of others when stress takes hold of the brain.

Neuroscientists at the University of California, Berkeley, have found that chronic stress triggers long-term changes in brain structure and function. Their findings might explain why young people who are exposed to chronic stress early in life are prone to mental problems such as anxiety and mood disorders later in life, as well as learning difficulties (University of California–Berkeley 2014).

Behavior

As a child's behavior escalates, it is human nature for the behavior of those around to escalate as well. However, when describing a problem behavior, those emotions and emotional descriptors only serve to cloud the real issue. When describing or documenting the problem behavior, it is critical to be objective and as specific as possible. Instead of saying the child was very angry, you might say that they slammed their fist on the desk and then pushed a chair over onto the floor. They screamed "I hate math!" and then went into the hallway for ten minutes. So, while they may have been angry, they might also have been frustrated or upset about an unrelated event. By keeping assumptions out of the description, the data can be more clearly analyzed and more useful for planning for prevention in the future. The key is to try not to include what you *think* they might be feeling and rather describe an accurate picture of what the behavior looked like.

It is also important in most cases to indicate the frequency, duration, and intensity of the problem behavior. To illustrate this point, consider the following real-life scenario.

A kindergarten student was demonstrating the following specific behaviors:

- Aggression in the forms of hitting, kicking, and screaming.

- The most common antecedents to the behavior were:

    - transitions from highly preferred to less preferred activities

    - not getting what he wants (e.g. not being allowed to finish an activity).

Over the course of four weeks, the data revealed the following:

- While the frequency of the target behavior(s) has remained almost the same, the intensity and duration of the behavior(s) has decreased significantly.

    - Duration has decreased from approximately 20 minutes per episode to two or three minutes per episode.

    - Intensity has decreased so that Dylan is able to resume positive behaviors much faster.

    - The intensity of the behavior itself has decreased in that he no longer screams or pushes back. In addition, he rarely falls to the ground when upset. And when he does fall to the ground, he stands up in a short amount of time when presented with a visual cue.

Clearly, frequency-only data would have indicated no progress. However, the intensity and duration data tell a very different story. While there is still work to be done, the plan is definitely working to build positive momentum.

Consequences

A consequence is the event that immediately follows a response or behavior. Given this understanding, then positive reinforcement can be a type of consequence. Providing positive feedback or a pleasant, preferred outcome as a result of a desired behavior is a way of using consequences to build positive momentum and teach more positive behaviors. Another example of a consequence after a less desired behavior that builds positive momentum might be to pause and intervene with a reminder or mini-lesson of what a preferable behavior looks like. This type of consequence scaffolds the child's development and recognizes that they are in the process of learning how to behave. By providing a consequence that is positive or instructive, the relationship between the adult and the child is more likely to be positive and influence future decisions.

Research by Marzano, Marzano and Pickering (2003) shows that positive relationships are the foundation of effective classroom management.

Of course, another type of consequence is the use of punishment. Punishment is often used in the name of teaching better behavior, but the impact is multilayered with possible unintended outcomes in the long term. *Research indicates that punishment is sometimes accompanied by significant negative side effects.* Martens and Meller (1990) have shown that students who are regularly the object of punishment may over time show a drop in positive attitudes toward school (resulting in poor attendance and work performance), have a more negative perception of teachers, and adopt a more punitive manner in interacting with peers and adults.

Moreover, *punishment* is only effective at deterring inappropriate behaviors in so far as it provokes fear in children. Children come to fear for their possessions (that they may be taken away), privileges (that they may be revoked), preferences (that they may be used against them) and even safety and well-being (if they are routinely caused pain or harm in the name of punishment). Children do not necessarily come to understand why their behavior was wrong, or how their behavior negatively impacted others. In contrast, the effects of *discipline* on children are often an increased sense of responsibility, self-confidence, and the ability to distinguish appropriate from inappropriate behaviors.

In those instances when punishment is used, it is important to add an element of reflection and/or instruction to rebuild the relationship and teach a better behavior.

Often, negative feedback or even punishment leads to feelings of failure or poor self-esteem. These negative feelings can actually cascade into more negative behaviors, the exact opposite of the intended outcome.

Logical consequences are those that allow students to learn from their mistakes while preserving their dignity.

Goals of logical consequences:

- To give children the chance to *regain self-control.*

- To help children *recognize the connection* between their actions and the outcomes of their actions.

- To allow them to *fix problems* caused by their misbehavior and to make amends.

- To guide students in *avoiding similar problems* in the future.

- To *preserve the dignity* of the child and the integrity of the group.

- To keep children *safe.*

Characteristics of logical consequences:

- Respectful

  - The teacher's words and tone of voice communicate respect for the student.

  - The focus is on the behavior rather than on the student's character.

- Relevant

  - The consequence is directly related to the problem behavior or actions.

- Realistic

  - The consequence must be something the students can reasonably do and that the teacher can monitor and manage.

The goal of discipline is to instruct, guide, and facilitate the development of self-regulation. This shift in thinking requires that adults view their role as model, teacher and coach with the goals of building children who realign their difficulties from within instead of relying on decisions by adults to manage those difficulties. Effective discipline accomplishes a great deal more than punishment ever could. While punishment may eliminate the behavior in the moment with the punisher, it does little to build internal systems and strategies for lifelong self-regulation. Discipline provides the following:

- provides feedback that is specific, objective, and reflective

- shifts the center of responsibility for the problem to the child as much as is possible

- offers support and guidance from adults

- takes the time to offer options for solving the problem

- teaches how to use resources to work through a problem in appropriate ways

- builds the relationship with adults and peers.

Yes, discipline takes time. I encourage you to think about how much time you are already spending on responding to and dealing with disruptive or inappropriate behaviors. Write this number down in minutes in the space below:

In the absence of a plan for prevention and effective discipline, this number may continue over time and may even increase. However, with a plan for prevention and effective discipline, the amount of time spent dealing with these behaviors will more than likely decrease over time. So while you will take time to discipline and build positive momentum toward positive behaviors, this time is perhaps the most valuable investment of time you can make for your children now and in the future.

Collecting and Analyzing Data

Data is an essential component to applied behavioral analysis, the science and study of human behavior. Through consistent and quality data collection teachers and parents will be better able to determine the antecedents and possible function(s) of the behavior. This is the key to building a plan for prevention and more positive momentum. Data will also inform whether the interventions have actually been effective and to what degree.

The reality is often that data is collected in a narrative or anecdotal format. Lots of writing means lots of time collecting the data and even more time analyzing the data for meaning. To clarify this point, let me take you on a classroom visit. When called upon to provide support to a classroom teacher who is experiencing a challenging behavior, I always ask to review any previous and current data as part of the process of building positive momentum. More often than not, I am presented with a large notebook with pages and pages of handwritten notes that describe how terrible things have been. While there has obviously been a lot of heartfelt work put into this notebook, it usually focuses primarily, if not solely, on the problem behavior. The antecedents and the effects of the consequences are usually missing. If we are to build a plan that will prevent future behavioral problems, then a clear understanding of the antecedents or triggers is the most important piece of the puzzle. Another problem with reams of anecdotal notes or narrative commentary is that I need to read through all of it before I can derive meaning that is useful and helpful to the process. So, less with the right ingredients is definitely more in this situation. The data collection form in Table 1.2 provides all the right ingredients or critical components of quality data collection.

Table 1.2 Data Collection: Behavior

Student: _____ Staff: _____ Date: _____

Time	Antecedent				Behavior			Consequence			Effectiveness
	Activity	Location	Description	Persons involved		Intensity 1 2 3 4 5	Length (sec/ min)			Other:	

Key: 1 = very low, 2 = low, 3 = moderate, 4 = high, 5 = extremely high

Getting Started

Let's take a moment to reflect on some common considerations that may contribute to the decisions that adults make in response to child behavior. Some of the below are true and some are false; see which on the next page.

1. Teachers reported more difficulty managing the behavior of high maintenance students and were observed to provide more negative feedback to them compared to those who were industrious.

2. Dynamic interactions between teachers and their students occur in elementary school on a daily basis.

3. Only boys engage in challenging behaviors. Especially boys with silver hair and a thunderbolt on their left elbow.

4. School-age students whose temperaments were low in task persistence, high in activity, and high in negative reactivity were likely to have negative interactions with their teachers and to exhibit disruptive classroom behavior.

5. Those whose temperaments were low in activity and negative reactivity, in addition to being high in task persistence, were perceived by their teachers as teachable and competent.

6. Teachers gave students whose temperaments were low in activity and negative reactivity, in addition to being high in task persistence, more positive feedback and perceived them as requiring less supervision.

7. Parents are the only cause of children's misbehavior. Especially parents with silver hair and a thunderbolt on their left elbow.

8. "You really are not working hard" is a statement of positive reinforcement because it gives a student the incentive to work harder.

9. Boys were more likely to receive positive teacher feedback than were girls. These findings are corroborated by other observational studies that found that girls receive little

attention from their teachers as noted by Kelly (1988) and Rudasill and Rimm-Kaufman (2009).

Answers: 1. True; 2. True; 3. False; 4. True; 5. True; 6. True; 7. False; 8. False; 9. True.

What Is the Significance of These Statements?

The most important consideration is that adult behavior has an impact on children's behavior. And that adult behavior may be influenced by certain variables such as gender, cultural background, and temperament. It behooves educators to recognize how these may be impacting their current actions and reactions toward certain students. Educators and parents have the ability to de-escalate a situation or guide toward a better outcome by how they choose to react to a situation. Imagine a game of tug of war with an adult at one end and a child on the other. Every time one pulls, the other feels the need to pull harder for fear of failure. However, if the adult were to simply drop the rope, then the child would not be able to further engage with more pulling. Rather, they would both have an opportunity to pause and develop an alternative plan to achieve the desired outcomes. Adults, after all, have already developed their social and emotional skills and are better equipped to manage these difficult times. How an adult responds to frustration or loss or failure can provide a positive model to a child who is still learning how to handle these stressful emotions.

> Children are great imitators, so give them something great to imitate. (Anonymous)

Keogh (2003) indicates that teacher training and professional development programs could be strengthened by emphasizing individual differences in temperament and the ways in which these differences influence children's adjustment to the social and academic demands of the classroom. McClowry *et al.* (2013) have shown that a temperament-based teacher and classroom program has significant promise for positively affecting young children's academic and social skills particularly for children who are shy or more prone to negative emotions, such as anger. The mechanism by which this occurs is through improvements in children's regulation skills; thus, teacher understanding of temperament and application of classroom management that is tailored to individual differences in temperament foster children's abilities to stop and think before acting.

If educators assume that parents are doing their best, that relationship has a greater chance to build a more cohesive plan for support for each child. In the absence of communication and support from the parents, educators still have the same job: to educate each child to the best of their own ability. It serves no purpose to put blame on others, but simply to move forward with the best intentions for the time that you do have to build positive momentum and take it as far as you can.

Families may struggle with many economic, medical, and emotional challenges. Children living in these circumstances may need even more understanding and support from educators. Their families may benefit from services and support as well.

TEACHER REFLECTION FOR STUDENT SUCCESS

Reflective practice is thinking about what you did, what the result was, and deciding what you would do differently next time. The ability to critically examine one's professional practice in a constructive manner is a healthy and rewarding component of effective teachers.

1. What went well today instructionally and/or behaviorally?

2. What could have gone differently today instructionally and/or behaviorally?

3. Was my response to a difficult behavior positive, instructive or punitive?

4. How could I have responded differently to this difficult behavior?

5. What do I want to remember and learn from today?

Expert teachers adjust their thinking to accommodate the level of reflection a situation calls for. Their teaching is characterized by an intentional competence that enables them to identify and replicate best practice, refine serendipitous practice, and avoid inferior practice. Because of their ability to reflect, great teachers know not only *what* to do, but also why.

Research by Constantino and De Lorenzo (2001) substantiates the role of reflection in teachers' professional growth. A disposition toward reflection should be part of all teachers' repertoires.

Chapter 2

LAYERS OF PREVENTION

The single best way to address challenging behaviors in young children today is to take steps to make sure that they never occur... PREVENTION!

It is important to keep in mind what we do want for our children as we address targeting challenging behaviors. By focusing on the behaviors that we do want our children to develop, the energy of teachers and parents can work toward these desired behaviors which will build positive momentum toward positive behaviors. Stay dedicated to those desired behaviors that build future citizens who are contributing and positive members of this world. Take each opportunity to teach how to:

- accept differences
- help others
- ask for help when needed
- solve problems peacefully
- advocate for your needs
- advocate for the needs of others
- share what you have
- take turns
- listen actively
- participate fully

- wait patiently

- support others

- take risks.

The following are key components to setting the stage for prevention. Remember, it is not an easy or quick fix and often requires multiple structures and strategies working together to build positive behaviors:

- Model Positive Behaviors

- Develop Authentic Relationships

- Set Clear Expectations

- Teach Expectations

- Provide Positive Feedback

- Build an Organized Environment

- Nurture Problem Solving

- Teach Self-Regulation

- Collaborate with Families

- Collect and Analyze Data.

In the past, reactive strategies tended to be the predominant response to the occurrence of challenging behavior. Increasingly, however, family members, researchers, and teachers have been seeking prevention-based and early-intervention strategies for creating proactive and positive environments for social growth and emotional regulation in young children

A. MODEL POSITIVE BEHAVIORS
Show Respect

Teachers model respect to students by listening to them and showing them that they care about things that are important to them. A sincere greeting in the morning can do a great deal to build relationships and also find out how a child is feeling as they start their day.

Teachers can apologize when they have forgotten to do something they said they would do, when they lose their temper, or when they make a mistake. A thoughtful teacher can even model how to use certain strategies when they are feeling frustrated. As an example, the teacher might share with the class that they are feeling frustrated by something and they need to go to the "Chill Zone" to take a moment to calm down and feel better. By taking two or three minutes to regain their own composure, the teacher models and reinforces the use of this area and related calming activities such as coloring, play-doh, or relaxation and breathing exercises. Teachers can also encourage respectful behavior through classroom discussions about how to show respect to others and what behaviors are disrespectful and why. There are often many opportunities throughout the day to stop and have these instructive conversations. Teachers should then consistently provide positive feedback to students when they do show respect or any effort to improve those skills.

Think Out Loud

To demonstrate how to think through a problem, teachers can think out loud. Teachers often use this strategy related to academic tasks such as demonstrating the solution to a math problem, where you tell students your thought processes as you're solving the problem. This same strategy may be applied to social and behavioral situations. Rather than just offer a solution, include the children in the process and encourage creative solutions that will benefit all involved. Ask guiding questions that will facilitate them to think about the pros and cons of the possible solutions. As teachers and children engage in thinking out loud to solve problems together, relationships are strengthened and lifelong skills are taught and developed.

University of Rochester psychologist Ed Deci (Ryan and Deci 2016), for example, has found that teachers who aim to control students' behavior, rather than helping them control it themselves, undermine the very elements that are essential for motivation: autonomy, a sense of competence, and a capacity to relate to others. This, in turn, means they have a harder time learning self-control, an essential skill for long-term success.

Know Your Children

It is imperative to know the strengths and needs of each child. Through parent conversations, observations, data collection, and time, teachers begin to better understand each child and what each child needs in order to flourish in all areas. One of the deepest ways to connect with another person is to get to know what they like and why. A person's interests are often related to talents or preferred activities and can be highly motivating in a variety of ways. If a child's interests are celebrated, they feel valued. If a child's interests are incorporated into their school day, they may feel more connected with the educational experience. If a child's interests are sprinkled throughout their day, they may even demonstrate more positive behaviors. As more strategies are introduced, keep the idea of sprinkling interests as a way to enhance the effectiveness of the strategy itself. A simple decoration of their favorite superhero or singer or Disney character on the strategy can make that strategy have meaning and a stronger personal connection. A feelings chart with a monster truck theme might make that feelings chart more relevant and more effective in teaching children how to communicate their feelings and having coping strategies when those feelings start to escalate. The student profile may be used to help gather information that is meaningful and useful for individual children.

⬇ Table 2.1 Student Profile

Student Name: _____ DOB: _____

Date: _____

Teacher: _____ Grade: _____

Campus: _____

Area	Strengths	Needs
Academic: • Literacy • Math • Science • Social Studies • Electives		
Social: • Peer Interaction • Problem Solving • Large Group Activities • Small Group Activities		
Communication: • Receptive • Expressive		
Additional Needs	**Circle any that apply:** Toileting Eating Self-help Mobility	
Student Interests:		
Parent Comments:		

Summary

Whether teachers and parents are fully aware of the impact of their words and actions, it is important to always be mindful of those ever-watching eyes. Adults teach every time they solve a problem in calm and respectful ways. Adults teach every time they share their feelings and pose solutions. Adults teach every time they deal with difficult tasks with confidence and effort. Children are watching and they are paying attention to the smallest of details. Adults bear an important responsibility in providing a model of those very behaviors that are expected of the children that they teach. Remember:

- Children watch and learn when you might least expect it.

- They watch how you treat other adults throughout the day.

- They watch how you treat other children as they misbehave.

- They watch how you treat them in good times and especially through struggles.

- They are watching and learning how to be to others.

B. DEVELOP AUTHENTIC RELATIONSHIPS

Trusting and affectionate relationships with caregivers during infancy and toddlerhood provide the basis for a healthy self-concept, confident exploration, and later positive relationships with peers and teachers (Thompson 2001). Research from the High/Scope Foundation (Schweinhart *et al.* 2005) indicates that the way adults interact with children plays a very important role in children's learning and development. These studies demonstrate that in classrooms where teachers are responsive, guiding, and nurturing, children take more initiative and are more likely to be actively involved and persistent in their work.

Body Language

Adults, by virtue of being adults, are typically taller than most children. Without trying to present an imposing or dominating figure, a towering adult can add stress from a child's perspective. Stress may be negative when a person feels threatened and not in control of the situation. These feelings instigate a powerful reaction, affecting both the brain and body in ways that can be destructive to physical and mental health.

Daniel Goleman (1997) further explains that "continual emotional distress can create deficits in a child's intellectual abilities, crippling the capacity to learn."

The same adult can communicate more effectively when the aspect of stress is minimized as much as possible, especially in challenging moments. By simply joining children at their physical level by kneeling or sitting, adults can send a message of togetherness and collaboration. This entry point to a discussion can change the dynamics from adult control to shared control and even problem solving. The interaction can be made more positive through open hands, a smile, and supportive looks.

Tone of Voice: Warmth and Affection

Effective communication is more than choosing the right words. Whatever is being said can be overshadowed by the tone of voice, the volume used, and other nonverbal cues like facial expressions and unsupportive body language.

The tone of your voice expresses understanding, acknowledgement, connection, and several other healthy things to children. Although your words are very important, equally important is the tone with which you speak those words. Everyone has been in the situation where the *real* message behind the words was received loud and clear thanks to the negative tone in which it was delivered. Sarcasm can ooze out and cover positive words in such a way that any positive intent is lost, leaving hurt feelings or even a damaged relationship.

C. SET CLEAR EXPECTATIONS

Classroom rules work best when students understand why rules exist and how rules will help them, as individuals and as a group. Gartrell (2010) reminds teachers that three or four guidelines work well in the elementary grades. Too many rules may complicate the issue unnecessarily and dilute the focus on the most critical expectations.

Examples are:

- We are friendly with others and ourselves.

- We solve problems together.

- Mistakes are okay. We just need to learn from them.

Remember to always state the rules in positive terms. While it may be tempting to remind students that there is to be "No hitting" or "No running" or "No screaming," these examples almost assume the worst and do very little for guiding the children toward the desired outcomes and behaviors. There are many fun examples of positively stated class rules on Pinterest and Teachers Pay Teachers websites. When possible, include the students in the development of the class rules. Most teachers are surprised by the innate understanding of children as to what is expected in order to have a well-organized and positively managed classroom. Children may even offer more extreme rules than a teacher might expect. Developing class rules together can create a sense of community and a common language for expectations.

Having class rules that are positively stated is only part of the process. In order for these rules to have an impact, they should be referred to and taught through practice and feedback. The morning circle time or morning meeting time is ready-made for reviewing the class rules on a regular basis and having lessons on following the rules. Rules may also be reviewed at the end of the day to reflect on how the class did that day. Class celebrations or motivating activities may be linked to positively reinforcing great days. Less great days offer an opportunity to reflect, teach, and practice rough spots.

Classroom Rules: Pitfalls to Avoid

When an adult enforces rules with children, the children know they have done something wrong. However, the negative experience in rule enforcement does not teach them what to do instead (Readdick and Chapman 2000); for example, "You know the rule, no hitting! Go to the time-out chair."

Busy with enforcement, adults easily forget the importance of teaching children positive strategies like using words or walking away as alternatives to hurting a classmate. Rules can cause teachers to label children, lump them in groups, and enforce rules accordingly: be lenient with the "good children," who mostly obey rules, and be strict with the "misbehaving children," who often break rules. Studies from Ladd (2008) show that children frequently subjected to punitive rule enforcement feel rejected, develop negative self-images, and may have long-term problems with aggressiveness in school and life.

Individual Student Supports for Class Rules

There are multiple ways to format visual supports to further clarify expectations for those students who benefit from something more personal, concrete, and interactive.

The smaller version of the classroom rules are called "keychain rules" (see Figure 2.1). They are provided for either each student in the classroom or for students who struggle with following the rules. They can be reviewed for prevention purposes and then can be easily referenced when a student needs a rule reminder. As with most strategies, personalizing the strategy with a highly preferred character or thing can increase the effectiveness of the strategy. Depending on the age of the child, they can keep their own keychain rules in a designated location or they could be located on a hook near the classroom rules.

There comes a time in every classroom when the noise level gets downright too loud. Before you know it, you find yourself having to raise your own voice just to be heard. "Quiet! It is too loud in here. I can hardly think with all the noise." Then the class gets quiet for a while until the next resurgence of sound and here we go again. This strategy can have wonderful results for individuals, but has much broader implications for the entire class as this is a common struggle among students, with or without special needs.

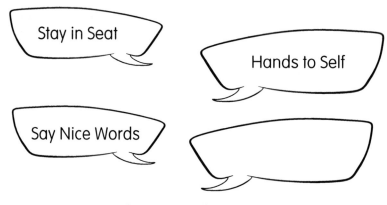

Figure 2.1 Keychain Rules

Let's start with how you might use a Levels of Talking Chart (see Figure 2.2) with the entire class.

1. Practice what each level sounds like to gain common understanding of the 1 through 4 meter or scale.

2. Make a poster of the Levels of Talking chart and place it in a prominent location easy for all to view.

3. Make a large arrow affixed to a paper clip or clothes-pin (or other creative way to move the arrow up and down the chart) and attach it to the poster.

4. Move the arrow to the desired level of talking at various times throughout the day.

5. Reinforce success by pointing to the chart and saying, "Thanks for staying at a 3 for this project!"

Another class-wide approach to using the Levels of Talking Chart is to place the expected level(s) at each center/station. For example, the Library Center might be at a 0 or 1 while the Science Center might be at a 2 or 3, depending on the activities involved.

A Levels of Talking Chart can also be used to further clarify expectations as they relate to noise level throughout the day.

Again, incorporate student interests and increase the relevance and motivation for students to follow the expectations.

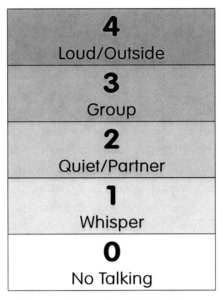

Figure 2.2 Levels of Talking Chart

D. TEACH EXPECTATIONS
Using Literature to Support Social-Emotional Development

Literature can be a fun and effective tool to teach and shape positive behaviors. Ann Marie Hamar describes the story of *Too Loud Lily* in the following way:

> Everything Lily Hippo does is too loud! She laughs too loud! She sings too loud! She even reads too loud! She is so loud that she wakes the baby at home and gets her friends in trouble at school. When a new teacher comes to Lily's school, she is asked to be in a play where she learns that there is a time and place to use her special talent (Ages 4–7). (Hamar 2004)

Activities that include the children in role playing and discussions about loud and soft voices can be used before, during, and after reading *Too Loud Lily* (Laguna 2002). An example of one activity may be to give each child a card with a "loud" picture (Lily yelling or cymbals crashing) on one side and a "quiet" picture on the other side before reading the book. Label each side of the card as loud or quiet. During reading, have all the children hold up their cards if they think it is a time for Lily to be quiet or loud as each page is turned. Continue the game throughout the daily schedule to teach students to self-regulate in a fun and relevant way. Hold up pictures of different activities across the daily schedule and let the children use their cards to show if they think they should be quiet or loud during that activity.[1]

By incorporating positive reinforcement and instructive feedback throughout the day, children learn to self-regulate and further develop positive social skills and behaviors.

Of course, some of the best sources of literature can be found in your own classroom. By having the children help create a story about positive behaviors, they have greater ownership of the story and ideas within. Adding photos of the students performing the desired behaviors and acting out the story makes the process even more personal and positive. One example of how a story might flow to help teach positive behaviors is as follows:

The First Grade Superstars!
We learn every day at school.
We work hard together and we have fun playing together.
Sometimes, we might have to share things like markers or cars or balls.
Sharing means taking turns with my friends.
When we take turns, we have fun together.
Sometimes, sharing might mean that we use the same toys together.
We are happy when we share together.
Friends try to take care of each other.
Sometimes, friends do not want to share all the time.
That is OK.
We can try to find another person to play with.
I can even have fun playing by myself.
I will try my best to take care of my friends. They are important to me.
The End

---

1   More activities using this book can be found at the following website: http://csefel.vanderbilt.edu/booknook/loudbilly.pdf

Now imagine this story with photos of the children acting out the story with big smiles on their faces. They become wonderful teachers themselves through this fun strategy.

Teachers can also use this type of strategy to help children be more successful and independent during transition times. As an example, a teacher took pictures of students as they completed their morning routine of getting ready for the day. She took pictures of them as they put their backpack away, moved their name to their preferred lunch choice, took their journals out, and got started writing on the prompt of the day. As children enter the class, these pictures are scrolling on a PowerPoint presentation to provide a clear visual cue of what the expectations are to start the day positively.

Another resource for promoting social and emotional competence can be found on the website for the Center on the Social and Emotional Foundations for Early Learning.

These modules are designed based on input gathered during focus groups with program administrators, early childhood educators, and family members about the types and content of training that would be most useful in addressing the social-emotional needs of young children. The content of the modules is consistent with evidence-based practices identified through a thorough review of the literature.

E. PROVIDE POSITIVE FEEDBACK

Research indicates that you can improve behavior by 80 percent just by pointing out what someone is doing correctly. Positive interactions can be provided in a variety of ways including verbal praise, nonverbal acknowledgement, non-contingent attention, and planned rewards. A high-five or a "thumbs up" can go a long way in nurturing a child's development and self-confidence. After all, confidence builds positive momentum toward positive behaviors.

Redirection or negative interactions are not wrong and are sometimes necessary; the key is the *ratio*. As noted earlier, the way in which a negative comment or corrective feedback is delivered is also important in how it impacts the relationship between the child and the student. To illustrate how important relationships are to the learning process of academic and behavioral skills, answer this question for yourself: You have two different people ask you to do the same thing for them. You have great respect and admiration for the first person and you like being around them. You have little to no respect for the second person and you run in the opposite direction when you see them coming. Do you respond to their requests to do the very same thing in the same way?

Of all the people that I have ever asked this question, they invariably admit that their response is different based on their feelings toward these two very different people. The relationship factor is what makes behavioral change as much art and humanity as it is a scientific process.

For every redirection or negative interaction, students should experience five positive interactions. This balance serves to provide corrective feedback while maintaining the best elements of a positive relationship.

- Positive reinforcement is a naturally occurring behavioral process that can increase the rate, intensity, duration, or form of a behavior.

- Effective teachers use reinforcement as a powerful tool to teach, shape, and encourage appropriate behavior.

- The goal of any reinforcement system is not to manage or control behavior, but to help students improve behavior and move students to intrinsic motivation and reinforcement.

Maag (2000) says that "adult attention, even if it is negative, is a powerful reinforce—especially for students with the most challenging behaviors who typically receive very little positive attention." This understanding should give pause to educators and parents as they provide corrective feedback.

The most challenging children often draw out negative feedback or comments from adults. However, this negative feedback may actually serve to further reinforce problem behaviors. When teachers can reflect on their own responses to individual children, they can better understand the power of those interactions and adjust for more positive outcomes. For those most challenging students, take some time to reflect on teacher and children interactions using Table 2.2.

Table 2.2 Positive Attention Data Sheet

Student: _____		Date: _____
Time/Activity	Positive Attention ☺	Negative Attention ✗
TOTAL		

My ratio of positive to negative is:

Insights:

Building Positive Momentum

Harry Wong (Wong and Wong 1998) has shown that for a child to learn something new, this needs to be repeated on average eight times. For a child to unlearn an old behavior and replace it with a new behavior, the new behavior must be repeated on average 28 times. While this may vary from child to child and situation to situation, there is definitely a strategic plan that needs to be put in place to build positive momentum toward positive behaviors.

Feedback

Take a moment and write some notes about how you might deliver feedback that has the following elements:

- specific and descriptive

- positive

- reflective

- encouraging

- open-ended.

Feedback Notes

When a child does not follow the class rules, a teacher can provide corrective feedback by saying:

When a child pushes another child on the playground, a teacher can provide corrective feedback by saying:

When a child blurts out consistently throughout the day, a teacher can provide corrective feedback by saying:

Celebrations

Celebrations can be used to provide positive feedback to individual students or to an entire class. Celebrations, such as the following, also provide a bit of reinforcement, movement and fun that build a sense of community.

> ➤ **Clam Clap**

> ➤ **Jalepeño**

> ➤ **Microwave**

> ➤ **Trucker Call**

> ➤ **Elvis Thank You**

> ➤ **Rollercoaster**

> ➤ **Seal Clap**

> ➤ **Sprinkler**

> ➤ **Eggbeater**

> ➤ **Fireworks**

> ➤ **Yee Haw!**

Figure 2.3 Celebrations

Directions for Celebrations

The directions for these celebrations are as follows:

- Clam Clap

  - Hold both hands up and open and close them as if they are little clams.

- Jalapeño

  - Pretend you are holding a jalapeño between your forefinger and thumb and bring it to your mouth. Bite the jalapeño (making a biting sound) and then wave your hand back and forth in front of your face saying, "Aye ya ya ya ya!" as if it tastes very hot!

- Microwave

  - Hold up one hand and ball it up in a fist except for the pinkie. Move the pinkie finger up and down as if it is waving by itself.

- Trucker Call

  - Pretend you are pulling the horn cord on a truck and say, "Honk, Honk," as you pull twice. Then bring a pretend hand radio to your mouth and say, "Good job, good buddy."

- Elvis Thank You

  - Pretend you are Elvis and you are holding a guitar. Then strum and swing your hips back and forth as you say, "Thank you, thank you very much."

- Rollercoaster

  - Pretend you are holding on to the rail of a rollercoaster and inch up as if it is rising to the top of a hill making a clicking noise. Once you are at the top, then swoosh down saying, "Wooooooooo!"

- Seal Clap
  - Put your arms straight out in front of you. Overlap them and turn your hands toward each other so that they can clap. Clap several times while making seal noises.

- Sprinkler
  - Put your right hand against the back of your head with your elbow pointing back. With your left arm straight out to the left, start clicking and moving to the right as if you are a sprinkler. When you get all the way to the right, move your left hand back to the left side, slowly making swishing sounds.

- Eggbeater
  - Stand up and swing your legs open and closed while you crank your arm as if you are a human eggbeater.

- Fireworks
  - Put your hands together in front of your chest as if they are forming a rocket. Then move them up while keeping them together in the air like you have launched a firework. When you get to the top, spread your arms apart and make an exploding noise.

- Yee Haw!
  - Slap your knee with your hand as you say, "Yeeeeehaw!"

Goal Setting and Positive Feedback

The train ticket strategy in Figure 2.4 encourages students to focus on a desired behavior stated in positive terms. When the desired behavior occurs, the teacher and student celebrate with a punch on the train ticket. Once the entire ticket is punched, the student then earns a reinforcing activity or thing. Restaurants use this strategy when trying to reinforce patronage, by giving punch cards every time someone buys an appetizer or other special item.

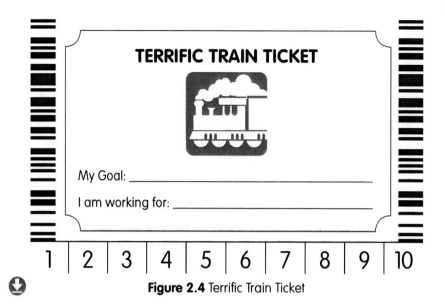

Figure 2.4 Terrific Train Ticket

The train ticket strategy may be modified to include a class or student interest. Student interests may increase the effectiveness of the strategy by connecting on a personal level. Remember to work toward goals and never take away something that has already been earned.

A goal-setting form can be formatted in ways to promote home and school communication that is positive and helpful. Notice that in the goal-setting form in Figure 2.5, the "Oops" category does not indicate a bad day, but rather a day to learn from. This can then be outlined more specifically in the last section, which asks the child to reflect on their day and indicate what they learned. This may focus on academic or social or behavioral learning, depending on the goals and outcomes of the day. Using "Oops" instead of a sad face can help children to feel more supported, especially when they know that their parents are going to see the form.

Name: _____	Date: _____

My goal:

| |

How did I do today:

Oops	OK	Very cool	Awesome

What did I learn today?

| |

Figure 2.5 Goal-Setting Form

Another example of goal setting and positive feedback is a well-planned choice board as you see in Figure 2.6. A teacher needs to determine what the desired activities are and then build a reward system that promotes the positive engagement in those activities.

In this example, the student is offered a choice of what they would like to earn and how they would like to earn their choice. For every part of their day that they perform all desired behaviors, they then check off that section of the bingo choice board. For instance, if the student wants to earn ten minutes on the computer, then he or she would need to demonstrate appropriate behaviors during the Daily 5 activities, Specials, Morning Carpet Time, and Centers, teachers always guiding and supporting toward better behavior all day, of course. This strategy is to scaffold the student as they build momentum toward more positive behaviors.

BINGO		
Choice Board		
Name: _____		Date: _____
1. Daily 5	**2.** Lunch/Recess	**3.** Morning Carpet Time
4. Morning	**5.** FREE	**6.** Cleaning Up
7. Specials	**8.** Play Centers	**9.** Math Centers

Bingo Prizes

A. _____ 3 in a diagonal row = 7 minutes on the iPad

B. _____ 3 in a horizontal or vertical row = 5 mins early to centers

C. _____ 4 corners = 10 minutes on the desktop computer

D. _____ Cover board = Treasure Box

Figure 2.6 Positive Choice Board

F. BUILD AN ORGANIZED ENVIRONMENT

Schedules provide individuals with an understanding of what is to come and what is expected. This knowledge empowers an individual to have a sense of understanding and security that leads to success and independence. The schedule is the backbone for many other strategies to connect, creating a network of effective preventive supports.

Children like predictability! So do many adults. What does predictability do for you and your stress level? Would you appreciate knowing what to expect each day? Would you like to know when special events are coming up in your life so that you can prepare for them adequately and without stress? Creating and teaching the daily schedule helps communicate to the children the organization of daily activities and events. Providing a predictable daily schedule helps *prevent* the occurrence of challenging behavior.

Therefore, designing effective classroom environments involves implementing consistent daily schedules. When implementing a daily schedule, consider the following points. Young children in particular may benefit from the use of photographic or picture schedules that provide concrete, visual cues of the scheduled activities and routines. In fact, children who are just beginning to learn language may actually need to have real objects included in their schedules.

For maximum effectiveness of the strategy, include a way to indicate completion of activities. For example:

- Turn the schedule page over.

- Put the schedule page in a finished pocket or location.

- Move an arrow or other visual cue along as activities are completed.

A teacher whom I visited was working with children who had some behavioral challenges. She shared with me that the children had become accustomed to the routine and that she did not think that was a necessary consideration for the classroom management issues she was experiencing. I asked her to try implementing an interactive class schedule for a couple of weeks and then let me know her thoughts. This is her response:

Using the classroom schedule interactively appealed to so many of my kids and clearly gave some of my worriers a feeling of control over the day. I had one posted—which I changed daily—but only referred to it every now and then.

Crossing items off as we go has been so powerful! (Deborah Dolan)

The content of the daily schedule may vary from grade level to grade level, but will always strive to strike a balance that keeps energy flowing in a positive direction with opportunities for rejuvenation.

When organizing a daily schedule, teachers may want to consider rotating large and small group activities, varying active and quiet activities, structuring a transition time in the activity, and placing the most difficult activity at a time when the children are most alert and attentive. It can also help to include a schedule within activities as well as across activities. For instance, if the activity has several components, the teacher may want to communicate to the children what will come first, next, and so forth by showing the child a sequence of visual cues (e.g., photographs, line drawings) that represent the different components of the activity. Again, this will communicate to the child what to expect. (Alter and Conroy, n.d.)

Studies have documented that schedules and routines influence children's emotional, cognitive, and social development. For example, predictable and consistent schedules in preschool classrooms help children feel secure and comfortable.

Ostrosky *et al.* (2008) have found that schedules and routines help children understand the expectations of the environment and reduce the frequency of behavior problems, such as tantrums and acts of aggression.

Activity schedules that give children choices, balanced and planned activities (small vs. large groups, quiet times vs. active times, teacher directed vs. child directed, indoor vs. outdoor), and individualized activities result in a high rate of child engagement. In addition, the duration of the play period can affect children's social and cognitive forms of play. (p.2)

Activity schedules help to break information down into smaller chunks that feel more doable. From larger activity schedules to smaller checklists, they each help to organize time and activities in a visual format.

- Have you ever gone to the grocery store with a list?
  - If so, does it help to better organize your grocery shopping?
  - Does it help you to stay focused on what you really need?
  - Don't most teachers want students to be better organized and focused?
- Do you check off your list as you fill up your basket?
  - If so, is it because it helps you to stay organized and know how much you still have left?
  - Do you get a small sense of accomplishment with each item checked off?
  - Don't most teachers want their students to stay organized and work toward a finished outcome? Don't most teachers want their children to feel a sense of accomplishment?

Take a few moments to reflect on your class schedule and organization and record your thoughts in the box below.

Time for Reflection
- I have a perfect schedule…yeah me!
- I plan to make the following tweaks:

- I plan to create and post a class schedule and it will be fabulous!

Surprise Cards

Surprise cards help children to handle anticipated and unanticipated surprises throughout the day. From fire drills to assemblies, surprises can be more positive with the support of a friendly surprise card. In this example shown in Figure 2.7, a teacher surveyed her students and incorporated the top interests in the surprise card to increase the effectiveness of the strategy.

Figure 2.7 Surprise Cards

Classroom Organization

Research indicates that the structure of the classroom environment, paired with planned instruction, supports the development of social-emotional skills as well as prevents behavioral issues.

Core features of a well-structured classroom as in Figure 2.8 include the following:

- clearly defined areas

- clearly labeled areas

- well-organized materials.

Figure 2.8 Class Structure

The first questions to ask yourself when designing any classroom are the following:

- What are my students' needs?

- What are my instructional goals?

- How can I minimize disruptive behavior?

- What key areas do I want to include to best meet my students' needs?

Key areas may include but are not limited to the following:

- Large Group

- Small Group

- Individual Student Areas

- Centers/Stations

  - Reading/Library

  - Math/Blocks

  - Science/Sand and Water

  - Social Studies/House, etc.

- Break Area

- Chill Zone.

Mapping Out My Classroom

Remember to start out with the non-negotiables within your classroom. Where are the electrical drops/outlets for printers, computers, etc.? Is there a sink or cabinets to consider? Where are the windows and how can I use those for the benefit of the children? Now, take a minute and map out your key areas with your students' needs in mind.

Draw a map of your classroom with specific key areas

Labels in each area further clarify the instructional and behavioral expectations for the area, as demonstrated in Figures 2.9 and 2.10. Students may participate in the labeling process. Areas should be clearly labeled in ways that students understand. The use of graphics or pictures always enhances the meaning and clarity of the label for young and older children alike. The use of color, labels, and containers can help to organize materials within each area.

Break Area

Figure 2.9 Example of a Label for the Break Area

Library

Figure 2.10 Example of a Label for the Library Area

Research by Quinn *et al.* (2000) indicates that well-arranged classroom settings reflect clearly defined spaces within the classroom that are used for different purposes and ensure students know how to behave in each of these areas.

In classrooms for younger children that will involve organization centers in which to promote play and positive interaction, and changing the materials in each over time can increase interest and motivation. Consider adding the following materials to the different centers throughout your classroom.

- *Block Center:* String/yarn, cardboard rolls and cans, magnets, farm animals, dinosaurs, pebbles, mirrors, play tools and belts, construction hats, rulers and measuring tape, floor plan, level, balance/scale, numbers and letters, sandbox, puppets/dolls, balls, trains, grocery bags.

- *Library/Book Center:* Puppets, recorder/iPad, books on tape, paper/pencils/markers, wipe-off board, author's chair, prop boxes, "reading glasses" (plastic glasses with the lenses popped out), newspaper/magazines, magnifying glass, magnetic letters, stencils, chart tablet, word-picture cards, pointers, envelopes, blank books/journals, cookie sheet with cornmeal to promote finger writing, zip lock bags with gel for letter tracing, stickers.

- *House Center:* Play television, washer/dryer, furniture, plants, refrigerator magnets, recipes, newspapers/magazines, towels, hats, mailbox, photo albums, materials from students' homes, books, wall calendar, place settings, menus.

- *Sand and Water Table:* Funnels, measuring cups/utensils, fossils, sand toys (buckets/shovels/rakes), water toys (boats/propellers/fish/marbles), letters, pans, people figures, cars/trucks, cups.

An Area May Be Designated as a Break Area or a Free Choice Area

While not every classroom must have a break area, think of the benefits of having a location to provide positive experiences while giving children the hope of a break from the academic and social stressors of their day. The break area is used to reinforce positive outcomes and provide a designated location for preferred activities. Some students may need more frequent reinforcement than others, but the location is clearly organized so that children can better transition between academic and free-choice activities. A timer is often helpful in setting clear limits for how long students stay in the break area before resuming the daily routine.

An Area May Be Designated as a "Safe" or "Chill" Zone

A chill zone can be a place for students to gain control in order to continue their day positively. The chill zone may include calming materials such as books, play-doh, fidgets, music, blocks, bubble wrap, etc.

The chill zone may be located in the general education setting as an interim strategy prior to leaving for additional support.

A chill zone is a preventive strategy that helps students work through their roughest moments. Please note that the chill zone is *not* a punitive time-out procedure. It is a place to go to regain composure and deal with feelings of frustration, anger or confusion.

Student interests may be incorporated into the chill zone in a variety of ways, such as the decorations and items provided.

The Inevitable Question...

"But what do you do when everyone wants to go to the chill zone *all day*?"

Consider the following:

- In most situations, the novelty of the "chill zone" reduces fairly quickly for those students who don't really need that level of support.

- Use literature to teach young learners about differences.

- Last, but not least, use "chill passes" or "break cards" to help set limits while promoting self-regulation and control. We will review the implementation of "chill passes" or "break cards" a bit later in this section.

Summary

Setting the stage for successful learning for all students requires planning with knowledge of student needs in conjunction with instructional and behavioral goals. Building positive momentum toward positive behaviors begins with a well-organized classroom.

- Ensure that all areas can be seen in full view of adults without barriers.

- Organize quiet areas farther away from active or noisy areas.

- Literacy can be incorporated throughout the entire classroom by adding books and related materials throughout all centers/areas.

- Provide places where children can go to be alone but still remain in full view of the adults.

- Define boundaries with furniture and floor coverings so children can tell where learning centers start and end.

- Avoid large open areas that may invite running and rough play.

- Equip the centers with materials that reflect the diverse backgrounds and needs of your students.

- Label shelves and storage boxes with printed labels and pictures so children can connect materials with labels as they put materials away.

Teachers can reduce the occurrence of inappropriate behavior by revisiting and reinforcing classroom behavioral expectations, rearranging the classroom environment, adjusting the class schedule or revising instructional activities based on student needs.

G. NURTURE PROBLEM SOLVING

Carol Dweck (2006), a professor at Stanford University, is dedicated to researching attitudes about challenges, mistakes, and efforts, and how adults influence those attitudes in children. Dweck emphasizes that by developing a growth mindset, people realize that through effort they can grow, learn, and effectively respond to their world. People with a fixed mindset tend to avoid challenges and fear failure and making mistakes—they don't want others to see them as failures or not smart. This attitude stems from a belief that ability is fixed and that effort is for people who can't perform.

Children don't have a lot of experience in solving problems independently, so their toolbox isn't particularly well stocked; with practice and support, their inventory grows.

Current research shows that social-emotional learning is a vital part of a young child's educational experience. It affects not only a child's readiness for school but also their *overall development as a person*. Thus, educators of young children should feel supported in their teaching practices that promote and encourage positive social experiences.

What is Social-Emotional Learning?

- *Emotional self-regulation and self-awareness:* Responding to experiences with an appropriate range of immediate or delayed emotions and recognizing and being able to control one's own feelings.

- *Social knowledge and understanding:* Knowledge of social norms and customs.

- *Social skills:* The range of strategies for interacting with others; assisted by cognitive development, especially perspective-taking and empathy.

- *Social dispositions:* Enduring character traits, such as curiosity, humor, generosity, open- or closed-mindedness, argumentativeness, and selfishness; shaped by innate temperamental differences and environmental influences.

The relationships that preschoolers form with their peers help to shape and guide their later interactions with teachers and fellow students as they begin elementary school. These habits form with lifelong implications.

Summarizing the research on cognitive-social integration and school readiness, child development expert Kyle Snow identifies several thought-provoking connections (Snow *et al.* 2007). For example, although the direction of the relationship is not yet clear, behavioral problems and reading difficulties appear linked.

Work-related skills (a subclass of social skills including paying attention to directions, participating in groups, and focusing on classroom tasks) are positively related to later academic achievement. Children with poor work-related skills have higher rates of special education, while having stronger work-related skills can buffer against socioeconomic risk factors in early learning.

Finally, research shows a young child's social relationships with other children and teachers can smooth the transition to kindergarten. A child's ability to form friendships leads to peer acceptance in the classroom, which, in turn, supports school engagement and emerging academic achievement.

At the same time, the more children establish close and conflict-free relationships with teachers, the more they "acquire the skills taught in school, maximizing the impact of instruction and deriving the most benefit from school" (Epstein 2009).

Kerr and Nelson (1989) and Newman, Davies-Mercier, and Marder (2003) found that teachers often assume that students can perform a particular behavior, but *research shows that many children with behavior problems have poor social skills, especially the ability to read social situations and conform to group norms for appropriate behavior.* Before assuming that a student is knowingly misbehaving, a teacher should discern whether the student has the skills and the knowledge to behave appropriately. To assess whether a student has the requisite skills for proper behavior, it is strongly recommended that teachers observe carefully whether there are any circumstances where the student can perform the behavioral skill at a level of success commensurate with their peers, and whether the student knows when and where the behavior is appropriate.

Problem-Solving Approach
High/Scope Foundation

The High/Scope Educational Research Foundation is an organization that has been dedicated to the education of young children. The approach is child-centered and based on research on how young children learn best. With a foundation of purposeful and meaningful play, High/Scope has outlined a process for children to learn as they develop their problem-solving skills. The following are the six steps for doing just that.

1. Approach calmly, stopping any hurtful actions.

    -   Place yourself between the children, on their level.

    -   Use a calm voice and gentle touch.

    -   Remain neutral rather than take sides.

    -   Set limits if necessary.

2. Acknowledge children's feelings.

    -   "You look really upset."

    -   The child may want to hold the object, and even feel strongly about that. However, the adult will explain that he or she will hold the object in question for everyone's safety while they work to solve the problem.

    -   Describe their actions.

3. Gather information

    -   Ask for information from each child and listen carefully.

4. Restate the problem.

    -   "So the problem is..."

5. Ask for ideas for solutions and choose one together.

    -   "What can we do to solve this problem?"

    -   Encourage children to think of a solution.

    -   Help clarify the details.

6. Be prepared to give follow-up support.

    –   Describe how they solved the problem.

    –   Give acknowledgment: "You solved the problem!"

    –   Stay near the children.

Remember that the investment of time toward teaching problem solving has many returns. The more that children practice problem solving, the more likely they are to become independent and require less adult time to help work through their difficult moments.

To further highlight the importance of problem solving as a lifelong skill, the following are steps for conflict resolution in the work place as outlined by the HR Daily Advisor:[2]

1. Clarify what the disagreement is about. Clarifying often leads to a better understanding of the perspectives of all involved. While clarifying is taking place, so is listening.

2. Establish a common goal for all parties. In this step of the process, individuals are asked to map out a desired outcome or ending to this problem situation. Seek to link common threads that will form this common goal.

3. Explore paths toward meeting the common goal. This may take some time to reflect, discuss, and negotiate options.

4. Identify possible barriers to this common goal. By under-standing the possible obstacles that may be encountered along the way, a plan for circumventing those problems can also be put in place for a smoother resolution.

5. Agree on the best solution to resolve the conflict. Although there may be several possibilities, ask for agreement on the solution that best meets the needs of those involved.

6. Restate the agreed upon solution and determine the responsibilities that each person has in the resolution.

---

2   http://hrdailyadvisor.blr.com/2013/06/24/6-steps-to-conflict-resolution-in-the-workplace

Do you notice similarities between the High/Scope approach to problem solving for young children and the steps toward conflict resolution for adults? The sooner we begin teaching how to work through problems collaboratively and positively, the sooner we help students acquire this fundamental and essential lifelong skill.

The more we work together to solve problems, the better we get at solving problems.

Offering Choices

Providing opportunities for students to make choices has been demonstrated to be an effective strategy for preventing problem behavior and increasing student engagement. By simply restating a directive as a choice, the child feels more empowered and in control of the situation. However, the adult is sharing this control by identifying what the acceptable choices are for the situation.

Verbal choices may prevent further escalation while empowering the student to have some control through decision making.

- "Would you like to work on this by yourself or with a friend?"

- "Would you like to get started on that here or on the computer?"

- "Do you want to think about it for a minute or get started now?"

As an example, a teacher told a student that it was time to stop playing and go to the restroom. The student told the teacher that she wanted to keep playing and did not want to go to the restroom. The teacher replied that she really needed to go to the restroom and this to and fro happened several more times with voices elevated and no positive outcome. The teacher paused for a moment and then remembered that offering a choice versus a directive might be an effective way to prevent further escalation and achieve a positive outcome. She then said, "Do you need two or three more minutes before we go to the restroom?" In this new interaction, the teacher offered a choice and also provided the expectation after the time limit had finished. The student first responded by saying that she wanted 100 minutes. The teacher said, "Oh, that's a lot of minutes! This time, you can have two or three. Which would you like?" The student thought for a second and said, "I'll take three." The teacher set the timer and when it rang, the student put her toys away and went to the restroom. The teacher helped the student be successful and also modeled how to work through a problem.

We get control by giving control.

Non-example:

> Choice Statement: "Do you want to go sit down or go to the office?"

Why is this a non-example?

That's right. These choices present one *real* choice and one more punitive option. This phrasing of a choice may actually further escalate a situation and even promote a loss of instructional time. This same choice, however, could be offered in a supportive way if the adult were to say, "Are you ready to sit down or do you need a short break first? Would two or three minutes in the chill zone help you out?"

A choice board can be used in conjunction with the break area or chill zone to help a student indicate what activity will help them to regain their composure and return to the expected activities. When the choices of reinforcing activities are offered in a visual format through the use of a choice board, students may be more likely to indicate what they need at that moment. As most individuals get upset or frustrated, they tend to become less verbal and may even appear to "shut down." Rather than asking for a verbal indication of the preferred activity, the student can simply point to the picture/word as a way to express their needs. And remember that you can always decorate the choice board with a student interest to increase the effectiveness, as in Figure 2.11.

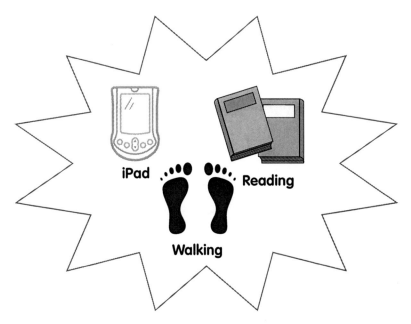

Figure 2.11 Calming Choice Board

Choice can take on many forms as related to academic tasks. As one example, students can be given several topics to choose from to complete an assignment. Students may also be given a list of several activities, of which they are to complete two. By giving them a choice, students are more likely to begin the assignment and are even more likely to complete it.

Making a connection to effective teaching practices, differentiated instruction promotes the use of choice in a variety of ways. At a center or station, students may choose from a list of five to six activities. These academic choices can be written on "I Can..." charts or other appealing formats.

For example, an "I Can..." chart at a math center or station may outline a list of choices of a variety of activities that would be engaging and motivating:

- Put a puzzle together.

- Play a game.

- Build a structure.

- Count the pieces in a puzzle to be sure I have all I need.

- Make my own puzzle.

- Make my own math game.

A science station might have yet another list of fun activities to choose from:

- Read about insects.

- Make and label an insect diagram.

- Write five facts about insects.

- Choose one insect and make a poster about it.

- Use a magnifying lens to observe an insect in the jar.

- Write about what I observe on a clipboard.

Remember, choice comes in many forms. Offering a choice of writing tool, "Would you like a pen or marker?" could make all the difference to kick start the learning process. Maybe even having a choice of where the activity will take place can increase a student's motivation. Many elementary classrooms have embraced the concept of flexible seating.

Flexible seating may offer choice within structure when there are some guidelines as to when and how this might occur.

Flexible seating options include:

- working at tables or traditional chairs with attached desktops

- standing at bookshelves or tall tables or ironing boards that can be easily stored

- sitting on gaming rockers or stools, or on carpet squares on the floor or outside on the ground (weather permitting)

- sitting or kneeling on pillows at low tables

- sitting on soft seating, beanbag chairs, or couches

- sitting on the floor in work nooks—corners created with bookshelves and walls.

We all like to feel in control, and making a choice is one way to exert control in an appropriate way.

Time to Stop and Reflect

- Do I have the following components in my classroom?

- What would I add?

- What would I revise/tweak?

  - Class schedule that is interactive.

  - Class rules/expectations posted and referred to.

  - Clear procedures.

  - Clearly defined areas.

  - Clearly labeled areas.

  - Well-organized materials.

  - Positive environment.

  - Student work displayed.

H. TEACH SELF-REGULATION

A feelings chart, as in Figure 2.12, can be introduced as a class-wide strategy to support children as they learn to self-regulate and manage their feelings and emotions.

Feelings Chart			
Describe		How I feel	What I can do
	5	I need some help!	
	4	I'm really upset.	
	3	I've got a problem.	
	2	Things are pretty good.	
	1	Feeling great!	

Figure 2.12 Feelings Chart

Implementing the Feelings Chart

A key feature to this, and almost any other, strategy is to teach and review it when the individual is calm and there is no problem at the moment. These conditions help to ensure that the brain is at its best, with most rational thinking, and that the strategy is not associated with a negative or difficult situation.

The start of the day is usually a good time to use the feelings chart as the person checks in to the school routine. Unless there has been a morning problem at home or on the bus, this is usually a time where there is a clean slate from which to build. Depending on the grade level, the feelings chart may be posted as a large visual guide of feelings, or as a personal tool in a notebook, or both. The calming activities may be reviewed along with some role-playing. By using the feelings chart first thing in the morning, the teacher can assess where the students are in their feelings and respond accordingly. Responses may include celebrating and reinforcing positive feelings and offering support to those who indicate a problem is developing. If there is a problem, then help the student refer to the pre-determined calming activities and identify which holds the most promise for resolving the situation.

A feelings choice board or feelings scripts may be helpful to understand how the child is feeling when they do reach a level of 3. They may be shutting down or unable to put their emotions into words at that time, but they may be more able to point to a picture or write down some words or draw a picture of how they are feeling and possibly why.

The feelings chart may also be used to debrief the day at the end of school. The chart may facilitate a conversation about what worked, what did not, and how to make a better plan for the next day. And remember to refer to the feelings chart when the student is calm and happy. The more we celebrate those moments, the more we focus on good times and positive energy.

When the student is calm, try to identify activities or strategies that will de-escalate once at the levels of 3, 4, or 5 on the emotion rating scale. Some possibilities may include:

- play-doh

- arm windmills

- breathing chart

- yoga moves

- wall push-ups

- counting chart

- coloring

- taking a walk.

Calming Strategies for the Brain

Consider the following categories when trying to determine the most effective ways to calm down and de-escalate from a situation. Learning how to self-regulate in the face of frustrating or angering situations is most definitely a lifelong skill.

The adult coloring book industry has tapped into the idea of coping mechanisms as a lifelong need. The prefrontal cortex is responsible for coordinating thousands of decisions each day, from which shoes we should wear to life-altering relationship and career choices. As an unconscious response to this so-called daily "decision fatigue," making a series of small, inconsequential decisions, such as teal or magenta for this squiggly line, may provide a refreshing sense of self-control after a long day of big, important ones.

When each of us becomes overly stressed or frustrated, we have all found a coping mechanism that helps to deal with the stress and frustration in more positive and healthy ways. Some of us may go for a walk, or sit in a candle-lit room with music, or do some gardening. Whatever your strategy might be, it probably falls into one of these three categories. Keep these in mind when identifying possible coping and calming activities for the children to engage in at school and even at home.

- Gross motor activity (e.g. walking, jumping, wall push-ups, arm windmills).

- Simple and repetitive task (e.g. coloring, play-doh, building blocks, reading, etc.).

- Soothing sensory experience (e.g. listening to music, visualization, breathing, etc.).

The chill zone area can be supplied with tools that will help the children engage in calming activities more effectively; for example, choice board as was previously mentioned, or a breathing chart as in Figure 2.13. By turning the page until they are calm, the child has a concrete tool that will help them focus and gain control more readily.

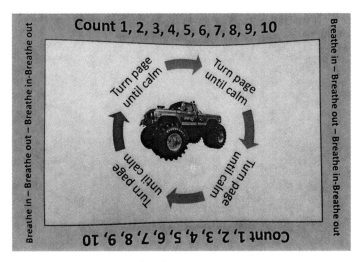

Figure 2.13 Breathing Chart

Now for the earlier question about what to do if students want to spend too much time in the chill zone. Chill passes are tools to help the student make a request to go to the chill zone when becoming frustrated with current expectations or a situation. The chill passes provide an alternative, more acceptable behavior to elopement or other disruptive behavior. When possible, offer different times on the chill passes to promote the connection between the level of frustration and actual need of time to deal with that frustration. It is also another way to empower children with choices.

The chill passes can either be cut up and placed in a designated location for the student to manage, or kept as a full page (see Figure 2.14). If kept together as a full page, then laminate so that the student can mark off when they request and take a break. This can be a great way to collect data on the use of the chill passes. At a quick glance, the teacher or parent can see how many have been taken over the course of the day for a total of how many minutes.

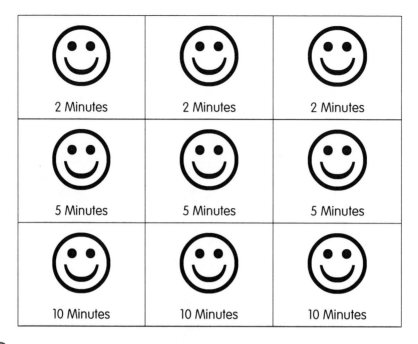

Figure 2.14 Chill Pass

Although it might feel like you are "giving in" to the student, this strategy actually teaches the student how to develop self-regulation and express their emotions with a more appropriate and safe response.

We get control by giving control.

Self-Regulation

Galinsky (2010) indicates that regulating one's thinking, emotions, and behavior is critical for success in school, work, and life. Bronson (2000) explains further that a child who stops playing and begins cleaning up when asked, or spontaneously shares a toy with a classmate, has regulated thoughts, emotions, and behavior.

When the components of executive functioning come together to determine behavior, this is called self-regulation. At its core, self-regulation is the ability to stop, think, and then make a choice before acting. Children demonstrate self-regulation in many ways: they stop and ask for what they want rather than having a tantrum, they take turns with friends while playing a game, they pay attention during a story, they wait in line, and they follow directions. The development of these skills best prepares children for school and beyond.

> Children who cannot effectively regulate anxiety or discouragement tend to move away from, rather than engage in, challenging learning activities. Conversely, when children regulate uncomfortable emotions, they can relax and focus on learning cognitive skills. Similarly, children experience better emotional regulation when they replace thoughts like "I'm not good at this" with thoughts like "This is difficult, but I can do it if I keep trying."
>
> Regulating anxiety and thinking helps children persist in challenging activities, which increases their opportunities to practice the skills required for an activity. (Florez 2011)

Blair and Diamond (2008) have stated that the process of moving from intentional to automatic regulation is called internalization. Some regulated functions, such as greeting others appropriately or following a sequence to solve a math problem, always require intentional effort. It is not surprising then that research has found that young children who engage in intentional self-regulation learn more and go further in their education.

Real-Life Implementation of Chill Passes

After looking at student data, it was determined for a particular student that four chill passes would be sufficient for the morning and four more for the afternoon. If she did not use her morning chill passes, then she could add them to the afternoon allotment, especially since afternoons were her most difficult time. Her four chill passes included one for two minutes, one for three minutes, one for five minutes and another for ten minutes. She quickly learned the concept of how to use the chill passes and would evaluate the situation carefully before deciding which amount of time she would need in the chill zone. For this student, the teacher also added the feature of combining her chill passes so that she could choose a maximum amount of time of 20 minutes in the chill zone at one time if the situation called for such measures. Remember that it is preferable to prevent a meltdown than to try to deal with a meltdown in full swing, for all involved. The staff decided that 20 minutes in the chill zone would be better than 40 minutes or more in a meltdown.

When implementing the chill pass at first, the teacher might need to read the student's signals and remind them that they have the option of using their chill pass if they need to calm down. A teacher or parent might say something like, "Remember that you can use a chill pass if you are feeling like you are at a 3 on the feelings chart," followed by, "How many minutes do you think you will need right now?" If the student has not used all their chill passes by the end of the day, they can be added to the next day's allotment, building up a bit of a "chill pass savings account." These could simply stay there for days where they may be more necessary or they can be exchanged at the end of the week for a reward or reinforcing activity, such as ten extra minutes on the computer or iPad.

What happens if the student runs out of chill passes before the end of the day in spite of everyone's best efforts? Then you can implement a policy of "borrow from tomorrow," much like dipping into your checking account deeper than you might like. While not optimal, it empowers the student to make the decision which will impact how many chill passes they will have for the next day. If they feel they need another chill zone time, then they will need to subtract one or more from their allotment for the next day.

A teacher working to support one of her students struggling with his emotions and self-regulation implemented a feelings chart. She shared with me that as she asked the student to indicate how he was feeling, he pointed at the smiley face on the "feeling great" level. She had sensed that he was not feeling so great, so she asked him why he pointed to that level and he explained that this picture was how he wanted to feel. If asked, I think most children would explain that they want to feel great. They may need some support, but together we can help all children achieve this goal.

In the space provided below, write down or map out your plans to implement the following preventive strategies based on your own students' strengths, needs, and interests.

Plans for My Classroom

- Break Area

- Chill Zone

- Feelings Chart

- Calming Activities

- Chill Passes

Goal Setting and Self-Evaluation: Feedback without Shame

- Why are publicly displayed behavior charts used in so many classrooms?

- What are the pros of these behavior charts?

- What are the cons of these behavior charts?

In a recent meta-analysis of more than 100 studies by Marzano *et al.* (2003), it was found that the quality of teacher–student relationships is the keystone for all other aspects of classroom management. In fact, the meta-analysis indicates that on average, teachers who had high-quality relationships with their students had 31 percent fewer discipline problems, rule violations, and related problems over a year's time than did teachers who did not have high-quality relationships with their students.

Imagine you're at work when you see it: your name on the wall, with a note from the boss that everyone can see. Your behavior is "unsatisfactory." We can think up different versions of this scenario. Maybe it's a simple visual message—your name pinned to a red traffic light. Maybe your deficiencies are communicated with a more positive spin—"We want to see you improve!"

But, either way, I'm betting you feel not so great. Your perceived shortcomings are being broadcast to the world, presumably to embarrass or shame you into changing your ways. Does it actually work like that—make you feel inspired to do better?

Or does the experience:

- Damage morale?

- Undermine your workplace relationships?

- Make you question whether you belong in this workplace at all?

Intuitively, it doesn't seem like a good approach to management, and Microsoft Chairman Bill Gates appears to agree. As he wrote in a recent editorial, "we would never have thought about using employee evaluations to embarrass people" (Gates 2012). And yet this approach continues to be widely accepted in schools today.

Consider what happens to you physiologically when you are singled out for disapproval or rejection. As you become conscious of the fact, your heart rate and blood pressure rise. Your body produces a surge of the stress hormone cortisol and your immune system responds by increasing activity that causes inflammation.

Even preschoolers have been tested and the results are sobering (Lewis and Ramsay 2002). *The more strongly four-year-olds felt shame, the more cortisol they produced.* Simple self-consciousness—like feeling shy about friendly attention—was also somewhat stressful. But it was knowledge of negative evaluation that made kids experience the highest cortisol levels.

And over the long term, these physiological changes appear to impair your health. In one study (Dickerson, Gruenwald, and Kemeny 2004), medical researchers found that patients experiencing persistent feelings of shame suffered a decline in t-cells, those front-line soldiers of the immune system that kill pathogens and tumors.

Therefore, we may imagine that kids who find themselves frequently shamed are going to be in a state of chronic stress and compromised immunity. What about their behavior, however? Isn't the idea that shame is supposed to motivate improvements, so the kids stop doing the things that get them into trouble?

Researchers like June Price Tangney (Tangney and Dearing 2002) have devoted their careers to understanding the effects of shame, and they see consistent evidence that shame, as opposed to guilt, has anti-social effects. When we feel guilty, we regret the effects our behavior has had on other people. We are often motivated to make amends. But when people feel shame, they feel so threatened they become desperate and defensive, a very different outcome. Their primary concern is to hide or deflect the blame, which often leads to anger. People may lash out at others or try to make someone else the scapegoat. Alternatively, they may try to minimize their shame by telling themselves they can't help it. They are just too incompetent, weak, or stupid to behave differently.

We've no reason to think kids are the exception. In fact, experiments suggest that young children are highly susceptible to criticism. When kids were asked to imagine themselves attempting a task and then being told by an adult, "I'm disappointed in you," the children experienced feelings of inadequacy. Instead of being motivated to improve their performance, they were more inclined to view themselves negatively and to give up.

And this was *without* an audience of other children. What might have happened if the children had been chastised in front of a class? Children who are perceived to be "in trouble" with the teacher are more likely to get rejected by their peers. The combination of public recognition of failings and rejection by peers can erode relationships and negatively affect a child's self-worth and even confidence. The very thing that educators put in place to teach better behaviors may actually contribute to the spiraling of students that struggle the most with the social and emotional development.

Things to think about:

- Have you ever noticed that the same students are always on a warning or lost privilege?

- Conversely, some students are always ready to learn and stay there consistently. What impact does this approach have on this type of a student? Are students who are intrinsically motivated to do the right thing systematically taught to rely on extrinsic motivation?

- If the same students are always on the warning or lost privilege level, then is this an effective strategy for changing behavior?

If the "pro" of a behavior chart is to provide specific feedback, then educators must ask if there is a way to do just that without a public display and possible shame.

When researchers were conducting those "I'm disappointed in you" experiments, they tested an entirely different, and beneficial, approach to correcting behavior.[3] And if you're a teacher eager to replace your classroom behavior charts with something else, consider personal goal setting and feedback forms. These strategies help guide children, scaffold their progress and provide a private and graceful way to recover and learn from mistakes.

---

3   You can read about it at www.parentingscience.com/correcting-behavior.html

Stage and Quiroz (1997) and Fitzpatrick and Knowlton (2009) have found that *self-management techniques* have been more effective in managing student behavior than teacher-mediated interventions.

Confidence

In response to external influences, people develop assumptions, some of which are constructive while others are harmful. One of these assumptions that can interfere with self-confidence and alternative ways of thinking is: "I must always have love or approval from every significant person in my life." An alternative response is: "This is an unattainable goal. It is more realistic and desirable to develop personal standards and values that are not completely dependent on the approval of others."

Strategies for Developing Confidence

- Celebrate successes.
  - Notice, recognize and celebrate efforts in meaningful and fun ways.
- Build on strengths and interests.
  - Know what students *can* do and capitalize on those abilities.
  - Know student interests and incorporate those throughout the curriculum.
- Provide a "safety net."
  - Know student needs and ensure that supports and strategies are in place to maximize the potential for success.
- Nurture generosity.
  - Create opportunities for students to contribute to the well-being of others.
- Practice self-evaluation.

- – Facilitate students to reflect on how they feel about their work, their play, their efforts.

- Facilitate problem solving.

  - – Support students as they work with each other to solve their own problems.

- Create joy.

What is Confidence?

- Confidence is the internal understanding that one is capable of being successful.

- Confidence is the element that thrusts individuals forward to attempt new endeavors.

- Confidence is the thought that one might succeed eventually, even if not at first.

People *with* confidence usually...

- have positive, yet realistic, views of themselves and situations

- trust their own abilities

- have a general sense of control in their lives

- believe that they will be able to do what they wish, plan and expect.

Persons *without* confidence usually...

- depend excessively on the approval of others in order to feel good about themselves

- avoid taking risks because they fear failure

- generally, do not expect to be successful

- often put themselves down and engage in self-defeating language.

Confidence builds success

Success builds confidence

Ways I can build confidence in my classroom...

Confidence

If you think you are beaten, you are
If you think you dare not, you don't
If you'd like to win but think that you can't
It's almost for sure that you won't.
If you think you'll lose, you've lost
For out in the world you will find
Success begins with a person's will
It's all in the "state of mind."
Life's battles don't always seem to go
To the strongest or fastest man
But sooner or later the man who wins
Is the one who thinks that he can.

(Author Unknown)

I. COLLABORATE WITH FAMILIES

Relationships between teachers and parents also play an important role in children's development. When staff and parents form warm, respectful relationships, they are better able to communicate openly about children's behavior and experiences and to respond to children's individual needs. In the context of mutually supportive relationships, parents are more likely to share information about family and home situations and stressors, and about their child's development and behavior.

They are also more likely to listen to and even seek the advice of school staff regarding parenting, child management, and discipline issues when they feel connected to and supported by staff. In addition, staff will have greater opportunities to become familiar with and responsive to the culturally based values, beliefs, and child-rearing practices of families.

The following are but a few ways to build relationships with families:

- Greet and share plans for the day.

- Include photos of families in class.

- Weekly/monthly newsletters.

- E-mails for quick updates.

- Phone calls/texts (within certain hours).

- Student portfolios.

- Share positive notes.

- Parent lunch dates with their children.

- Daily/weekly communication notebook.

- Class web page.

Webster-Stratton and Taylor (2001) have found that the use of harsh, punitive discipline strategies in the home is associated with the development of problem behaviors, and can lead to escalating cycles of coercive interaction between parents and children. Therefore, outreach to families and training/information on how to positively teach children how to behave benefits the home and school settings.

Materials and instruction addressing the development of positive, consistent behavioral strategies can assist parents in establishing routines that foster positive interactions and promote healthy social-emotional development. Parents can encourage the expression of positive emotions, empathy for others, and emotional self-regulation, as well as friendship and social problem solving skills in their young children through modeling and the ways they interact and discipline.

I plan to connect and communicate with my families by...

J. COLLECT AND ANALYZE DATA

From learning activities to transitions to social interactions, children's challenging behavior can influence every aspect of a classroom. Hemmeter, Ostrosky and Corso (2012) have found that teachers of young children report feeling concerned and frustrated about classroom management. Furthermore, Stormont, Lewis and Covington Smith (2005) discovered these same teachers often feel underprepared to address challenging behavior proactively.

These concerns are justified for several reasons. Dunlap *et al.* (2006) and McCartney *et al.* (2010) have found that children who frequently exhibit challenging behavior may have fewer friends or lower academic performance, and research links the persistent challenging behavior of young children to more serious behavior problems and negative consequences as they get older. Crick *et al.* (2006) continue by revealing that young children who demonstrate difficult behavior are more likely to face persistent peer rejection and negative family interactions and to be disciplined by school professionals.

But just as behavior can affect all aspects of a learning environment, all the aspects of a learning environment can be structured to promote positive behavior. By taking a few simple steps to collect data in their own classrooms, teachers can learn valuable information about behaviors occurring and how to better prevent those behaviors from developing into habits over time. Using simple forms like tally sheets or checklists, teachers can document which times of the day children tend not to follow expectations, whether children are engaged or off task during free play, and how long transitions between activities take.

Teachers can then use the data to make decisions that support positive behavior more effectively. For example, teachers can collect class-wide data to learn which expectations children find difficult to meet and to identify when and where challenging behavior is likely to occur. They can also collect individual student data to better understand the function of the behavior as stated at the beginning of this book.

Decisions that are based on data help educators to create the ideal learning conditions for students and prevent behavioral difficulties. Of course, every teacher is always struggling to find time to collect data but can do so in very creative ways. For example, placing a handful of paper clips in one pocket and transferring one paper clip to another pocket every time a behavior is observed is a relatively simple strategy that can be used during instruction. In addition to the multiple data collection apps now available, there are a variety of user-friendly forms that can be found at the Positive Behavioral Interventions and Supports website.[4]

Behavioral Shaping

Once again, keep in mind that behavioral change and development will take time. Depending on where the child is in their own behavior, small steps should be considered progress and celebrated along the way. These small successes are all building positive momentum toward ultimate, more long-term goals of positive behaviors. Behavioral shaping involves the following components:

- Teach the behavior by modeling, prompting, and supporting.

- Reinforce the behavior that is close to the desired behavior, then raise the criteria for reinforcement in small steps until desired goal is reached.

Positive Reinforcement

Positive reinforcement is the presentation of a specific stimulus after the expression of a particular behavior that is desired. The positive reinforcement increases the likelihood that the desired behavior will continue and that the child will tend to adopt it as a habit.

These are many types of positive reinforcement, including *concrete reinforcer*, *social reinforcer*, and *activity reinforcer*.

- *Concrete reinforcer:* This is something that is very concrete and tangible.

---

4   www.pbis.org

- *Social reinforcer:* This may be a simple gesture or form of celebration.

- *Activity reinforcer:* This is a positive opportunity to engage in a fun or interesting activity.

When possible, include the student in identifying and selecting positive reinforcement. Be sure to pay attention to signs of satiation and be ready to change as needed to maintain the positive behavior(s).

Prevention

Teaching behavioral expectations, providing reinforcement and support, and monitoring are essential components to the *prevention* of challenging behaviors. Doolittle (2006) has also shown evidence that administrative support, communication, and data-based decision making were found to be the most important characteristics for long-term sustainability.

While it takes a wise person to solve a problem, it takes a wiser person to prevent the problem before it ever happens.

The following are possible strategies for preventing behavioral difficulties and increasing student success:

- *Antiseptic bouncing:* Remove the student from the situation without calling attention to a specific behavior (e.g. "Let's take a walk," "Please take this box next door," "Time for a drink of water," etc.).

- *Positive practice:* Provide an opportunity to practice the skill and provide verbal feedback immediately.

- *Offer assistance:* Rather than emphasize the completion of academic tasks in spite of obvious frustration, offer assistance and assess the situation to make instructional adjustment(s).

- *Active listening:* Listen to the student and paraphrase back to clarify meaning and validate a need to be heard.

- *Preemptive prompting:* Remind student(s) of appropriate behavior *before* the activity takes place.

- *Help cards:* A visual cue that indicates that the student needs assistance. The card may be raised or turned over as a way to request assistance.

- *Break cards:* A pre-determined number of cards that the student may use to request a break for a certain amount of time. These cards can have varied amounts of time on them so that the student can assess the situation and self-regulate accordingly.

- *Chill pass:* Provide a specific number of "chill passes" that will prevent further escalation. The "chill pass" may be used to go to a specific location in the general or special education classrooms.

- *Journaling:* Use journaling for self-expression and reflection.

- *Behavioral momentum:* The teachers deliver a set of easy requests before asking the student to engage in a difficult task.

- *Incorporate interests:* Interests can be powerful motivators when used purposefully throughout the day. Interests can be incorporated throughout academic tasks, identified as an incentive or positive reinforcement, or even "sprinkled" as decorations on strategies.

- *Visual supports:* Refer to a visual strategy that will help the student perform the desired behavior (e.g. keychain rule, T-Chart, Social Story, choice board, feelings chart, etc.).

Classroom Implementation

The following is an example of using a combination of antiseptic bouncing, interests, and visual supports to prevent elopement out of a kindergarten classroom. The student is new to the school and has never been to school before. He has tried to leave the campus twice in his first week of school and both times the most obvious antecedent (trigger) has been engaging in a large group activity where all the children are together on the carpet. Specialists have been called upon to collect more data through observation and parent interview to better determine the cause of the elopement behavior. In the meantime, the class teacher is trying to keep her students engaged in meaningful instruction and positive behaviors while maintaining the safety and well-being of all her children.

While visiting this class, I collected information using the student profile that captures student strengths, needs, and interests. I took this knowledge into consideration when determining how to intervene in a situation to prevent elopement and build positive momentum. I observed the child go to the carpet for a large group activity when instructed to do so, but then he quickly started to crawl toward the back of the room in the direction of the door. The teacher also noticed the move toward the door and she proactively moved to stand in front of the door and block his exit. However, this response escalated his behavior to that of head-butting the teacher's legs. Although the intensity was fairly low, it was not appropriate and indicated a possibility for further escalation.

With my limited knowledge of his strengths, needs, and interests, I decided to intervene firstly with antiseptic bouncing. Remember that antiseptic bouncing involves removing a student, in a non-punitive fashion, from the environment or immediate situation in which the difficulty is occurring. At school, the child may be sent on an errand. At home, the child may be asked to retrieve an object for a parent. During this time, the student has an opportunity to regain a sense of calm. Upon returning, the problem has typically diminished in magnitude and the adult is prepared to provide further support, if needed.

This strategy is most effective when the student is in what is called the "rumbling stage." Rumbling may be evident by fidgeting, clenched fists, loud talking, increased breathing, head down, and any other sign of stress, anger, or concern. The signs will, of course, vary from person to person. Communication between home and school can help to identify those rumbling signs.

Often, staff need to communicate among each other to agree upon antiseptic bouncing strategies in advance. For instance, one teacher may be designated to receive a random note or box of pencils as one way to have a student be removed from the classroom to run an errand. The intent of the errand is to stop further escalation, not to run an actual errand. Antiseptic bouncing can be especially effective for students that do not respond well to any type of attention as they begin to be frustrated or angry.

So, in this moment of an escalating behavior problem, I fought the urge to say something like, "Stop that! You are hurting someone else. That is dangerous behavior!" Yes, this behavior needed to be addressed. Just not right then and just not in this way. Instead, I said, "Excuse me. Can you show me your top three favorite Skylanders characters?" He looked up and said, "I know everything about Skylanders!" I told him that was great and that we could sit together and use my phone. So far, I had used antiseptic bouncing and his interest to de-escalate the situation fairly successfully. But now what?

While he was looking for his top three characters to share with me, I started thinking about the next step toward more positive momentum. I decided to add a visual support to transition back to the classroom activities. I knew that the class was doing a whole group activity on the carpet called "Brain Pop." I also knew that they were going to do some activity that they had started the previous day after Brain Pop. I decided to try to get him to do those two activities and provided positive reinforcement by way of a little more time looking and talking about Sklyander characters.

I could have simply told him what to do next, but remember that words are transient and visuals are static. A static visual tool, such as a map, is more friendly to the brain than a string of verbal directions. This is especially true in times of stress and so I wanted to support my words with a visual. On a blank sheet of paper, I wrote down the following:

- Brain Pop
- Activity
- Skylanders.

Three simple steps and one highly preferred activity to look forward to. I reviewed the brief list with him and within a few seconds he joined the group at the carpet for Brain Pop. After the activity is finished, I told him that he had done a great job of completing that activity and that it was time to check off that activity in the box. As you can see in Figure 3.1 in the next chapter, the student had a different idea. He said that the whole activity was over and that he should fill in the entire box. Sounds good to me!

Then, he participated in the next activity, which involved cutting and pasting items related to a science project. He participated fully and positively in this activity and then a sudden interruption happened. The teacher looked at the clock and said that she had lost track of time and it was time to go to recess. She directed the students to put their materials down and line up. She reassured them that they could finish upon returning. "But that is not what is on my magic checklist!" I thought to myself. I anticipated the worst and prepared for another back-up plan to prevent any unravelling of our positive momentum.

Instead, this student carried out a pretty sophisticated form of self-regulation with this very new strategy by filling in a small part of the box. I asked him why he filled in a small part (as you see in Figure 3.1) and he explained that since he finished a small part of the activity, he should fill in a small part of the box. He paused his activity, had a great time at recess and returned to complete the entire activity. Now, it was time for more looking at and talking about Skylanders characters.

Of course, this is not the end of the story. Later in the day when all was calm, the teacher debriefed the situation with the student and drew pictures of what happened and discussed why this was not safe. Together, they drew pictures of two alternative ways to deal with frustration. And yet, additional assessment was to be gathered to determine the full extent of his educational and behavioral needs.

How can a simple checklist be so effective for even the most challenging behaviors?

A checklist does three things that help individuals feel that the undoable is more doable.

A checklist...

- breaks a task down into small chunks

- does it visually

- sprinkles in an interest when possible.

Summary

We will be exploring these and other strategies in the upcoming chapter. As we leave this chapter it should be noted that everything from this point forward builds on all that has been discussed so far. The foundation needs to be strong in order for any specific strategies to be effective. A strategy or technique by itself can only do so much in a chaotic or unpredictable environment at school or home. Once you have built a strong foundation through classroom organization, a classroom interactive schedule, class rules, instruction on those rules, positive reinforcement, and more, then you are ready to add specific strategies that will prevent either class-wide or individual problem areas.

The science of building positive momentum toward positive behaviors is grounded in applied behavioral analysis and supporting research. When a teacher modifies an antecedent to prevent a behavior from occurring in the first place, that teacher is applying a key principle of applied behavioral analysis. When a teacher uses data to make decisions about how to modify the antecedents to a behavior and prevent it from occurring in the first place, that teacher is applying another key principle of applied behavioral analysis. When a teacher uses data to determine whether or not the preventive strategy is effective, that teacher is applying yet another key principle of applied behavioral analysis.

The art of building positive momentum toward positive behaviors is grounded in yourself: your tone, your warmth, your supportive approach to solving problems together. Your modeling of kindness and how to be a contributing member of your school. And keep your genuine humor ready to build bridges, heal hearts and even diffuse a rough moment.

After all, a hearty laugh has been found to also elevate your mood, decrease stress and even boost your immune system.

Teacher: What do you want to be when you grow up?

Kindergartner: A dinosaur.

Teacher: [Smiles and chuckles.]

Chapter 3

BUILDING POSITIVE MOMENTUM

The first step toward building positive momentum is to try to determine why the student is demonstrating this behavior. Use Table 3.1 to identify the best guesses based on your data.

Table 3.1 Function of Behavior

Student:	Date:
Teacher(s):	
Behavior:	
Frequency:	
Duration:	
Intensity (1–5):	

Check all possibilities	Possible reasons behind behavior My best guess is…
	1. Need for attention from teacher
	2. Need for attention from students
	3. Need for movement/fun

cont.

	4. Need for control
	5. Sensory processing differences
	6. Lack of self-regulation
	7. Lack of instruction
	8. Lack of understanding
	9. Poor self-image
	10. Special education need
	11. Special medical need
	12. Other:

BEHAVIOR A: GETTING OUT OF SEAT... WITHOUT PERMISSION

Attention Span and Children

Sousa (2006) reported that most students will have a normal attention span of approximately one minute for each year plus or minus four minutes. It is important to provide students with an activity change or brain break before they reach the end of their attention span. Usually off-task, wiggly, disruptive students are signaling that their attention span has expired.

Consider the following possible strategies or supports to prevent excessive movement or getting out of their seat without permission.

- *Alternative seating:* From wiggle cushions to bean bags to cube chairs, alternative seating can provide just the right structure and support to stay engaged and focused on the task at hand. In some situations, simply allowing the child to sit away from a group of students may actually help them to attend better. You will know if this is an effective strategy when the child or children participate to a greater degree.

- *Fidgets:* There are a variety of fidgets available through many outlets. From spinners to squeeze balls to thera-putty, there is quite a business building around the need and usefulness of fidgets. Something as simple as a pipe cleaner can also be effective as a fidget. One student even asked to bring his to library with him, which is usually a tough time for him. Just having the pipe cleaner in his hands helped him to focus during an entire story. This is an example of how a child can be empowered to understand their needs and advocate for themselves.

- *Class rules:* If staying in their seat during certain times of the day is an important part of the class expectations, then it should be stated clearly as a class rule. The difficulty is that the conditions in which staying in your seat is an expectation often change. For instance, children are encouraged to walk around the room and engage in different learning experiences during center/station time. So, the rule applies some of the time, but not all of the time. Because of this inconsistency, the teacher needs to decide exactly what she does expect from the children and develop rules that are based on those expectations in clear and explicit terms.

  Review the class rules as a form of prevention and then they can become more effective references to remind children of the expectations. A personal set of those rules can be placed on a keychain for children who need a little more concrete support. Be sure to number the rules so that you can promote self-regulation by simply asking a child to check rule #3 as a way to remind and redirect discretely.

- *Props:* By bringing in props that children can hold and use in activities, their level of focus and engagement is increased. This is especially true when connections are made between the props and the instructional focus. Some examples of simple props include scarves, musical instruments, wipe-off boards, items from a prop box, glasses with the lenses popped out, pointers, etc.

- *The "dancing square":* A very creative teacher decided that she was tired of competing with students who have a need to express themselves as they are moved to do so. Rather than redirect them back to their chair or spot, she decided to sanction the need for random expression with a "dancing square" placed just off to the side of the carpet. Using electrical or duct tape, you can quickly mark off an area where children are encouraged to go to when they feel the need to move. In this classroom, the teacher made four small squares anticipating that everyone would want to go to the "Dancing Square." As with most strategies, the novelty wore off after a few days and only two of the students used it on a regular basis.

We get control by giving control.

- *Song choice board:* A song choice board can increase student interest and motivation in participating in the large group activities. The song choices can also be organized on a strip to indicate the order of the songs to provide additional structure.

- *Incorporate music and/or movement:* There are a variety of ways to incorporate music and movement to enhance the learning process. The following are but a few resources to continue to add to your own:

    - Go Noodle at www.gonoodle.com

    - Cosmic Kids Yoga Adventure Series on YouTube

    - Jack Hartman Series and Brain Break on YouTube

- *Positive behavior flip book:* A positive behavior flip book has universal appeal in that it talks in pictures to all the children with consistency and predictability. As you start to build this strategy, you want to think of the most common requests you make verbally on any given day and make sure they are included in the flip book. You can adjust your template by changing the pictures provided, adding new pages and/or deleting current pages. Once you have chosen your pages, then organize them in the order that you like. Now you can cut the tabs to fit your sequence, making each page have one tab that is easy to view at a quick glance.

   The positive behavior flip book can help to organize companion strategies such as a "first/then" board, surprise card, and even a "levels of talking" chart. Remember to use the visual strategies to reinforce appropriate behaviors. An example of this might be to use the positive behavior flip book when you see appropriate behaviors and show the visual as you give positive feedback.

- *T-chart:* The T-chart may be used to clarify acceptable or desired behaviors versus unacceptable or undesired behaviors, as in Figure 3.1. When possible, generate both lists with the students. If student input is not possible, then collaborate with support stuff and parents to identify what might be most essential to clarify. For younger children, pictures may enhance the effectiveness of this strategy. Refer back to the T-chart when the undesired behavior occurs. Practice replacement behaviors from the acceptable options outlined on the other side of the T-chart. The T-chart may be posted in the class or located in a student folder/notebook or both.

My T-Chart for:
Staying in My Seat

Not Quite Right ✘	Way to Go! ☺

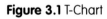

Figure 3.1 T-Chart

Example of a T-Chart in action:

Casey was a young fourth-grade student who loved to bring toy guns to school. Each day the teacher struggled to have him put the toy gun in his backpack once he had brought it to school. This item was not acceptable for the safety and security of all other students at this school, even in toy form. On some days, the debate about the toy gun took up much of their instructional time.

The teacher introduced the T-chart strategy to clarify that this was not an acceptable item to have at school. As a matter of fact, on the very first day the teacher asked which side the toy gun belonged on, and Casey looked at the T-chart and said "at home." Once they wrote it down, it seemed to become "the law." From time to time, he would still try to take the toy gun out of his backpack. The T-chart reduced the debate by taking a moment to refer back to this strategy.

- *Get out of seat cards*: For students that present a greater challenge in staying in their seat, personalized "get out of seat" cards may be helpful to develop self-control within limits. By providing a certain number of "get out of seat" cards to a student, they become more aware of how many times they are getting out of their seat and they also become more responsible for regulating their own behavior by managing the cards. Just like chill passes or break cards, the cards can be cut up and given to the teacher each time the student gets out of their seat without permission. They can also be kept on one page that is laminated so that the student can check them off as they are used. As the end of the day, the teacher and student can have a reflective conversation about how many were used and how the strategy is working for the student.

We get control by giving control.

BEHAVIOR B: TATTLING

Teachers of young children are often faced with the challenge of what seems to be an endless parade of students reporting as they are trying to teach. Figuring out how to deal with what we commonly call "tattling" can take a significant amount of time and energy and, as a result, teachers are often tempted to tell children to keep problems to themselves.

While perhaps well-intentioned, discouraging tattling creates more problems than it solves. It leads to a "culture of silence" in our schools and sends children disheartening and confusing messages: "Adults say they care, but they won't listen to my problems. If I tell when someone does something bad, I'm being bad, too. I'm alone here; no one will help me."

Such inadvertent but powerful messages clearly work against the culture of emotional and physical safety we want to establish for our children. Frequently we see reports of school officials who uncover bullying and learn that many students knew of prior incidents involving the same children. But the witnessing children told no one, and their silence emboldened those experimenting with bullying to go even further. We are often surprised by children's silence in these cases, but we shouldn't be. Often, they are simply following the "no tattling" rule they learned at home or in school at a young age.

Rather than tattling bans, educators need to develop a more nuanced view of tattling, along with ways to help children understand when and how to report problems.

Why Do Children Tattle?

There are many different reasons why students "tattle." Here are the most common ones:

- *Legitimate concerns:* Students may have good reasons for concern about others' behavior and its effects on them and their friends.

- *Need for information:* Some children may be testing the limits or trying to figure out whether adults will enforce the rules consistently.

- *Wish for attention or recognition:* Some children want adults to notice them or to acknowledge their efforts at following the rules. With their regular reporting and need for constant affirmation, these children can often interrupt the flow of instruction.

- *Limited problem-solving skills:* Adults often tell students to handle problems themselves, but students may lack the skills to do so. Tattling may be their only problem-solving strategy.

Replacing "Tattling" with "Telling"

Encourage children to report significant events—those that threaten someone's emotional or physical safety. Assure students that if they're uncertain whether an event is significant, adults want them to speak up. Help children develop independent problem-solving skills and resiliency.

Be sure to clarify the difference between telling and tattling in ways that your children can understand. Often, adults assume that children know the difference but just can't help themselves from tattling on their friends. For many children, they are just reacting to a situation without really thinking through their actions as not appropriate. A positive discussion about the difference between telling and tattling is the starting point to better understanding and building positive momentum toward better behavior.

You might begin by exploring students' prior understanding of tattling, followed by sharing your own perspective.

"I know that some teachers and maybe even your families have told you that tattling is not a good thing. While that is sometimes true, I want you to know that there will be some times you should tell adults about things that have happened that you are worried or concerned about. Today we'll begin talking about how you'll know when to tell the difference."

Help students know when to tell you about incidents that are important. Brainstorm common events that students report to you as a class activity. Put these incidents on index cards, perhaps in picture format for younger children, and then sort them with students using a chart with two columns, labeled "Tell an Adult" or "Work it out with a Friend." If you implement a journal for tattling, then you might add another column that directs the children to write it down in the tattling journal if they are unsure. This will be sure to provide a safety net for those situations that children have difficulty interpreting.

Possible ways to describe the main differences may include the following components:

- "Telling" is when you have tried to solve the problem yourself, and still need some help.

- "Telling" is when you are worried about someone else and want to be helpful.

- "Tattling" is when your goal is to get the other person in trouble.

Strategies to decrease tattling and increase positive reporting of concerns include:

- *T-chart:* A T-Chart, which we discussed earlier, may help to clarify the difference for children more explicitly. The chart may also be used when unplanned situations arise as a way to determine whether they are telling or talking.

- *Positive attention:* As a prevention strategy, give students positive ways to get your attention, especially if you suspect the tattling is derived from a need for attention. Also consider giving them a unique responsibility in the classroom, spotlighting them at morning meetings, or writing them the occasional note letting them know you've seen their positive efforts or accomplishments. He or she might be in charge of selecting the class celebration from time to time.

- *"Tattle tickets":* Tattle tickets may be another way to minimize the amount of tattling, while promoting self-regulation. Each teacher can decide how many tattle tickets to give to each student per day. As an example, each child may start out each day with one tattle ticket. At the end of the day, they can put their ticket into a basket if it was not used for tattling. At the end of the week, the tattle tickets can be added up to earn certain incentives, such as extra recess time, free dance time, free choice time, etc. The incentives may even correlate to the class percentage of tattle tickets saved or not used. If 100 percent of the tickets are saved, then the most prized incentive is what is earned and so forth.

- *Problem solving:* By teaching a process for solving problems as stated previously, children are less likely to have a need to tattle or tell. They will be more equipped to work through their problems with each other, even our very young three-, four-, and five-year-olds. Above all, children need to know that when someone's behavior worries them, adults will listen. Learning is not interrupted when we teach children how and when to voice their concerns. Such teaching increases their feelings of safety and also the possibility that we really can fulfill our responsibility to keep everyone safe in school.

BEHAVIOR C: TALKING OUT OF TURN (AKA "BLURTING OUT")

Many students have difficulty controlling their impulses, especially as they relate to talking out randomly or blurting out answers in class. In small doses, these behaviors may not present too much of a disruption to the flow of the class; however, when these behaviors occur frequently and excessively, the focus and attention of the entire class may be impacted negatively to varying degrees. Here are some strategies to help clarify expectations and set limits on blurting out.

Positive Behavior Flip Book

Effective teachers help children know when it might be acceptable to share without raising hands and when it is not. After all, there might be times where a teacher actually encourages the free exchange of ideas. But then, the expectations may change within the course of an activity and students can be confused.

Have you ever been enjoying a group discussion where all the students are contributing their ideas without raising their hand and having a great time. Then, it gets a bit too loud and you then say, "OK, remember to raise your hand" as a way to bring down the noise level. It can be difficult for students to navigate and self-regulate this behavior when the expectations change, sometimes without warning.

Adding pictures in the positive behavior flip book, which clarify when it is time to raise your hand to speak versus an open class discussion, may help students respond more positively to the teacher's expectations for any given activity.

Talk Passes/Blurt Out Cards

Talk passes (or blurt out cards) are designed to set limits on a specific behavior while empowering the individual to have a sense of control and self-regulation.

The student is given a certain number of talk passes (or blurt out cards) either for the class period or the day. Upon talking (or blurting out), the student gives up one of the talk passes (or blurt out cards) to the teacher. So how many cards should you give at first? In order to determine the best number of cards to give each student, collect baseline data to see how many times they are actually talking off task or blurting out. It might feel like 200 times, but it could actually be more like 15. If it is 15, then start with a number that would be attainable and build success with the strategy. If the student is blurting out 15 times, then the teacher might give 11–13 cards to gradually decrease the frequency. It is a wonderful thing when a student counts out how many talk passes (or blurt out cards) they have left before deciding to speak! This strategy develops self-control by setting limits and putting control back in the hands of the student...literally. The role of the teacher feels much more supportive: "Thanks, do you have any cards left?"

If the student runs out of talk passes (or blurt out cards) before the end of the class or day, you can institute a "borrow from tomorrow" policy. The child starts to manage their behavior with more reflection and self-regulation when they are part of the problem-solving process. Collect data and make a plan with the student to reduce the number of talk passes (or blurt out cards) gradually. Feel free to incorporate the student's interest to increase the effectiveness of the strategy.

As with tattle tickets, any unused blurt out cards can earn incentives once they are added up. A greater number of blurt out cards saved or unused can equal more special rewards.

Thinking Journal

Note pages decorated with a student interest can be used to jot down thoughts (words and/or pictures) during the morning meeting or other instructional times.

BEHAVIOR D: WORK AVOIDANCE

When addressing work avoidance behaviors, it is essential to try to analyze the reasons behind the behavior.

Is the work truly too difficult for the child? If so, then instructional strategies that clarify, scaffold or differentiate through technology may be effective. Perhaps the child could benefit from more hands-on instruction or "I need help" cards to prevent frustration

Is the work too simple for the child? If so, then incorporating a choice of more challenging activities may be effective—perhaps a choice board that incorporates activities that are both challenging and of high interest to that student.

Is the child easily distracted? Is the child more interested in social endeavors? If so, then perhaps a checklist with a choice board can increase focus and attention.

So, depending on the reason for the work avoidance behavior, teachers and parents will want to collaborate to build instructional success that will lead to behavioral success.

I Need Help Cards

"I need help" cards can provide support to students as they feel frustrated or overwhelmed with tasks, whether they be academic or otherwise. Even if a student is very verbal under most conditions, they may struggle with verbal expression when frustrated.

Another system for students to indicate a need for assistance is the stacking of colored cups.

- Green = I got this.

- Yellow = I'm struggling, but trying.

- Red = I need help now.

Chunking with a Checklist

For some students, a simple checklist, as in Figure 3.2, is all that's needed to get them started, build momentum, and keep them moving through academic activities. A checklist helps to make a difficult task feel more doable by:

- breaking it down into smaller chunks

- doing it visually

- sprinkling an interest.

These three simple components are highly effective for most students. By having a way to check off items as the student completes activities, there is a sense of accomplishment and the motivation of getting closer to a break, a preferred activity, or moving on to the next part of the day. And a simple decoration of a preferred character or thing can increase the effectiveness of this strategy.

Subject _____

Check
when done

1st

☐

2nd

☐

3rd

☐

Next: _____

"Way to go #15!"

Figure 3.2 Checklist

However, other students may need a bit more support to be successful. Here are some considerations to increase the effectiveness for these students:

- *Add a motivating activity at the end of the checklist:* Remember to encourage the students to check off the activities as they are completed. This can increase independence and provide a sense of accomplishment.

- *Use a "sandwich" technique of strategically placing simpler, or more preferred activities at the beginning and end of the checklist:* When the student sees an activity that they would like to do at the beginning of the list, they are more likely to get started. Once they have checked off the first activity, then they are to proceed to the next. Although this might not be a preferred task, they can easily see that another activity that they do like is soon to follow.

- *Add an element of choice:* You can do this by having the student choose three of the four activities on the checklist. This allows them to have some control over their academic activities while still holding expectations of completing academic tasks. Another way to provide choice is to have the student decide the order in which they complete the checklist. When you go to the grocery store, you might skip around the list, but you still get everything that you need by the end of the shopping list. The same idea applies here.

Mini-Map: Left to Right Checklist

For some children, especially those who are younger, a checklist in a different format may be more effective. A mini-map includes the same elements as a checklist, but takes a left to right format that is more interactive. The mini-map looks more like a small easel with pictures of the activities in a left to right sequence. As they are completed, the pictures are then moved to the back of the easel to indicate completion. Some students respond best to having a more concrete way to interact with strategies.

Instructional Scaffolding

Instructional scaffolding is a process through which a teacher adds supports for students in order to enhance learning and aid in the mastery of tasks. The teacher does this by systematically building on students' experiences and knowledge as they are learning new skills. The example of instructional scaffolding in Figure 3.3 is to support understanding of different punctuation. Some students may have difficulty determining the appropriate punctuation as this requires first understanding what the sentence is saying. The "If...Then" bridge serves to connect the necessary understanding in a visual format.

If...		Then
This is a question	Asking something	**?**
This is a statement	Saying something Telling something	**•**
This is said with	Excitement about something	**!**

Figure 3.3 Instructional Scaffold

Research

Visual scaffolding is a strategy for teaching students that utilizes drawings, photographs, imagery, and other visuals in order to help students to better understand the language and concepts within instruction. Alber (2014) notes:

> Using visuals for on-the-spot scaffolding (for an individual student or for the group) is unquestionably a best practice. Research shows that the population is made up of 65 percent visual learners. And only 10 percent of students are auditory learners yet 80 percent of instruction is delivered orally (University of Illinois 2009).

Pre-teach Vocabulary

Pre-teaching vocabulary involves introducing the words to children in photos or in context with things they know and are interested in. Use analogies and metaphors, and invite students to create a symbol or drawing for each word. Give time for discussion of the words to build relevance and make meaning. When possible, include photos of the vocabulary words in their own environments at school and at home.

Visual Aids

Visual aids such as graphic organizers, pictures/photos, graphs and charts can all serve as scaffolding tools. Graphic organizers are very specific in that they help children visually represent their ideas, organize information, and grasp concepts such as sequencing and cause and effect.

When used as a scaffolding tool, the completion of a graphic organizer is not the goal but rather a support that helps guide and shape the students' thinking. Many students benefit from using a graphic organizer when presented with a difficult reading selection or new information in any subject area that may be more challenging.

Kinesthetic Activities

Kinesthetic activities involve active learning and the use of large muscles when possible. As one example, if students are learning about a step-by-step process, consider writing each step out on a piece of paper and then placing the pieces of paper in order on the floor. The student can then physically walk through the process to have greater impact and meaning.

By placing a number line on the floor, children can walk up and down when adding and subtracting. By placing a large keyboard on the floor, children can "type out" spelling words with a partner. These kinds of activities not only increase meaning, but also provide an outlet for movement related to instruction.

A kinesthetic representation incorporates a body movement that helps understand and retain a concept. As an example, if I want children to remember that the brain remembers best when the body is involved, I might rub my head and then shake my body as I say, "The brain remembers when the body moves." With enough repetition, the kinesthetic representation will trigger the concept/message taught. The more we use nonlinguistic representations while learning, the better we can think about and recall our knowledge.

Mnemonic Devices

Mnemonic devices are patterns of letters, sounds, or associated ideas that aid people in remembering information. These mnemonic techniques use acoustically linked proxy words to connect two pieces of information. For example, students were given the keyword "rainy day" and told to think of a frog sitting in the rain to remember that the scientific classification for common frogs is ranidae.

Incorporate Technology

When the purposeful use of technology in the classroom is seamless and thoughtful, students not only become more engaged, they begin to take more control over their own learning. The following are but a few ways to incorporate technology throughout instruction across content areas:

- PowerPoint

- project-based learning

- Kidspiration

- learning videos

- ebooks

- interactive websites

- web quests

- voice recording

- virtual math.

Instructional Choices

When teachers offer instructional choices, they decide on the goal of the lesson or activity, then give students a list of options for what to learn and/or how to go about their learning in order to reach the defined goal.

The choices may be organized in a choice board or an "I Can..." chart as discussed previously. Plan choices based on the general abilities of your class, and structure them according to the goals that need to be achieved. Activities may include a wide range of options, such as writing reports, writing a comic strip, outlining a flow chart, acting out a passage, watching videos, or listening to educational audios.

Incorporate Student Interests

Student interests can be powerful in connecting the learner with the learning at hand. When a student is interested in the topic they are working on, there is no greater motivator. When possible, incorporate those interests throughout instruction in fun and creative ways. A math lesson just using Mario and Luigi characters to add and subtract may increase student engagement and motivation. Writing about a topic of choice can bring forth a wealth of knowledge about the topic and a desire to learn more about this.

Just Playing

When I'm building in the block room,
Please don't say I'm "just playing."
For, you see, I'm learning as I play,
About balance, I may be an architect someday.

When I'm getting all dressed up,
Setting the table, caring for the babies,
Don't get the idea I'm "just playing."
I may be a mother or a father someday.

When you see me up to my elbows in paint,
Or standing at an easel, or molding and shaping clay,
Please don't let me hear you say, "He is just playing."
For, you see, I'm learning as I play.
I just might be a teacher someday.

When you see me engrossed in a puzzle or some "playing" at my school,
Please don't feel the time is wasted in "play."
For you see, I'm learning as I play.
I'm learning to solve problems and concentrate.
I may be in business someday.

When you see me cooking or tasting foods,
Please don't think that because I enjoy it, it is "just play."
I'm learning to follow directions and see the differences.
I may be a cook someday.

When you see me learning to skip, hop, run, and move my body,
Please don't say I'm "just playing."
For, you see, I'm learning as I play.
I'm learning how my body works.
I may be a doctor, nurse, or athlete someday.

When you ask me what I've done at school today,
And I say, "I just played."
Please don't misunderstand me.
For, you see, I'm learning as I play.
I'm learning to enjoy and be successful in my work.
I'm preparing for tomorrow.
Today, I am a child and my work is play.

(Author Unknown)

BEHAVIOR E: DIFFICULTY WITH TRANSITIONS
Checklists

Checklists, once again, may be used for any activity that presents a challenge for the student. For example, a checklist may support a student who has difficulty with the steps of the morning routine.

> Starting the Day at School
>
> a. When I get to school, I will first open my backpack.
>
> b. Then, I will take my folder out.
>
> c. Next, I will put my yellow folder in my chair pocket.
>
> d. The last thing to do is put my backpack on the hook.

Now, add some pictures of each step and you have a helpful visual tool to promote student success and independence. Checklists can be created for any difficult transition such as getting ready for lunch, entering the classroom, walking in the hallway, and packing up at the end of the day.

Transition Songs/Cues

Most transition songs are sung to traditional and familiar tunes. Just change the words to relay the message and instructions.

Welcoming Song (Tune: "If You're Happy and You Know It")

I'm so happy to see you today,
I'm so happy to see you today.
(Child's name) won't you stand,
And shake your neighbor's hand.
Now everybody clap and say hooray!

Circle Time (Tune: "Oh, My Darling Clementine")

Time for circle, time for circle,
Time for circle time today.

Let's sit down, let's be quiet,
Wonder what we will do today?

Wiggles Out for Quiet Time (Tune: "Jingle Bells")

Clap your hands, stomp your feet,
Wiggle all around.
Reach your hands high in the air
And now let's touch the ground.
Hold your hips, hold your head
Give yourself a hug.
Sit right down, eyes to look,
It's time to read a book.

Clean Up Time (Tune: "Twinkle, Twinkle Little Star")

We've had lots of fun today,
It's time to put our things away.
We need all the girls and boys,
To stop now and pick up toys.
We've had lots of fun today,
It's time to put our things away.

Good-bye Song (Tune: "Are You Sleeping")

School is over, school is over,
Time to go home, time to go home,
I'll see you tomorrow, I'll see you tomorrow,
Bye, bye, bye; bye, bye, bye!

For older students, more contemporary songs can be used for the tune. As an example, the tune from the *Frozen* song "Let it Go" can be used with the words "Time to Go..." as a transition song out of the classroom or at the end of the day. As a class activity, take some time to have groups create songs for different transition cues. By giving the students this responsibility, their enthusiasm and ownership of these cues becomes enhanced. The groups can create songs for the following possible transitions:

- Get your materials.

- Line up.

- Get back to your seat.

- Finish up your work.

- Time for lunch.

- Start the day or good morning.

- End the day or good-bye.

Attention Grabbers

Teachers of young children have come to learn the effective use of fun attention grabbers to help increase attention and focus when needed and to indicate upcoming transitions. Instead of saying, "OK everybody, listen up," over and over, the teacher says a fun phrase that the students learn to respond to in unison. Introduce a few at the beginning of the year and then continue to add more throughout the year to keep the novelty factor up. The following are but a few attention grabbers to add to your menu:

- Holy Moly—Guacamole.

- Hocus Pocus—Everybody Focus.

- Hands on Top—Everybody Stop.

- Macaroni and—Cheese.

- Macaroni and Cheese—Everybody Freeze.

- Pepperoni—Pizza.

- Peanut Butter and—Jelly.

- Pop—Corn.

- My Bologna has a First Name—It's O-S-C-A-R.

- Ready, set—You bet!

Hallway Transition Cues

Scenario A: The teacher is taking her class to lunch through the hallways. Most of the children are walking as if they are pure and full of grace. Two students, however, are talking and falling out of line. The teacher stops the line, raises her voice and tells the students to stop and get back in line with her "teacher face" on that is looking angry, disappointed, and tired. The line resumes for another five feet when another student messes up the beauty of the line yet again. They stop and receive another reprimand. This happens five or six times to the destination. I won't even go into the transition out to recess! Sound familiar?

Scenario B: A teacher is taking her class to lunch through the hallways. She has instructed her students that they are "Spies." They are supposed to try to go down the hall so quietly that no one will know they are there, just like a spy. She shows them how to tip toe past doorways and duck under windows. She gives a big "Whew," wiping her hand across her forehead when they reach the destination. Smiles are seen up and down the line, including the teacher. You probably have your own creative way to focus students to walk quietly down the hallway in fun and kid-friendly ways. Here are just a few more ideas:

- Slither like a snake with your hands moving to and fro.

- Waddle like a penguin quietly.

- Walk like an elephant moving your trunk back and forth.

- Swim like a fish.

- Give yourself a big hug as you walk.

- Walk with a shark fin on your head.

- Walk like a chicken.

BEHAVIOR F: MINE, MINE, MINE!

Recommendations from the Institute of Education Sciences recognize that:

just as poor academic performance can reflect deficits in specific academic skills, some students' failure to meet behavioral expectations reflects deficits in specific social or behavioral skills. And just as explicit instruction can help students overcome some academic deficits, explicit instruction can help students learn the positive behaviors and skills they are expected to exhibit at school. Showing students how they can use appropriate behaviors to replace problem behaviors and consistently providing positive reinforcement when they do so can increase students' chances of experiencing social and behavioral success. (Epstein *et al.* 2008, pp.7–8)

Positive Teacher–Student Interactions

Positive teacher–student interactions are at the heart of building positive behaviors, including social skills. Studies conducted by Pekrun *et al.* (2004) linking positive emotions to achievement show that joy, hope, and pride positively correlate with students' academic self-efficacy, academic interest and effort, and overall achievement. Epstein *et al.* (2008) further note:

> Teachers show the warmth, respect, and sensitivity they feel for their students through small gestures, such as welcoming students by name as they enter the class each day, calling or sending positive notes home to acknowledge good behavior, and learning about their students' interests, families, and accomplishments outside of school. Teachers also can help students develop peer friendships by having them work together, thereby learning to share materials, follow directions, be polite, listen, show empathy, and work out disagreements. Fostering students' social and emotional development can improve their interactions and attitudes toward school, thereby reducing problem behaviors. (p.8)

Sharing Cube

A sharing cube may be introduced in a small group activity to promote an understanding of how it feels to share in a structured situation. Each child rolls the cube and then role-plays sharing the item or thing that the teacher has previously gathered for props. The teacher facilitates the interaction with specific feedback that helps to shape the behavior of sharing. Choose common things that children have shown difficulty sharing in the past, along with some fun options. Some possible things children can share include:

- toys
- crayons
- books
- cars
- smiles
- snacks
- blocks.

This explicit instruction in a structured setting will promote the understanding of the goal or desired behavior so as to increase generalization to other, real-life situations. Adults should be ready to provide support and feedback as children build positive momentum toward more positive behaviors throughout the day.

Narrative or Short Story

A narrative, or short story, may be effective in clarifying a situation and providing ideas on how to deal with that situation positively. Some of the most effective stories include photos of the students themselves telling a story.

The following narrative for teaching how to take turns at circle time can be enhanced with photos of the students performing the different activities.

TAKING TURNS AT CIRCLE

My name is _____ and I am _____ years old. I go to school at _____.

We do many activities at school like work, play, eat snack and have circle time. During circle time, we do lots of different

fun things like listening to books, dancing to songs and
_____. At circle time, friends get to help with
jobs like _____ and _____.
I really like to help with different jobs. There are lots of friends in
our classroom who also like to help with circle time jobs.

Sometimes I will get to help with jobs like _____
and _____ and sometimes it will be someone
else's turn.

If I really want to help and I don't get chosen, I can say, "Maybe
next time."

If it is someone else's turn and he/she chooses something I
don't like, I can say, "Maybe next time." If a kid chooses something
I like, I can give him/her a big thumbs up!

Circle time is fun when we all take turns!

While the stories can help teach almost any behavior, they can
also celebrate student success and provide positive reinforcement
as behaviors are acquired. When made in PowerPoint format, the
stories can be projected for the entire class to see and they can be
printed and placed in the class library for quick and easy reference.
They can even be sent home to families as a way to collaborate
and reinforce specific goals. There are also several apps, such as
Creative Book Builder, that can help create stories in fun and
friendly formats. Be sure that you have permission from all the
parents to use their child's photograph for this purpose.

The following resources provide narratives or short stories for
your consideration:

- Head Start Center for Inclusion: http://headstartinclusion.
  org

- Kansas Technical Assistance System Network (TASN):
  www.ksdetasn.org.

BEHAVIOR G: MY SPACE, YOUR SPACE…BODY AWARENESS

One of the ways that children start to demonstrate self-regulation
is through the understanding of spatial awareness. This awareness

involves specific language about directions and specific concepts of what this looks like in everyday life. My body moves and impacts others in the world when I play in many ways. This is a concept that often needs to be explicitly pointed out and clarified.

Teaching Body Awareness

Body awareness is the foundation upon which children learn to coordinate their body parts and move through space and about objects in their environment. Some children need practice to develop a better understanding of their body in relationship to others and the world. Teachers can help children develop better body awareness with activities that emphasize identifying body parts and how they work.

- The "Robot Game" is where the child pretends to be a robot and the teacher gives directions, such as "turn right," or "stop at the carpet," or "turn left."

- The "Freeze Game" helps children to transition from movement to stillness while also responding positively to directions.

- "Simon Says..." is another standard for developing body awareness and self-regulation.

Visual Cues

Some students may benefit from more explicit instruction through visual clarity as in Figure 3.4. Including the students themselves in the pictures can increase the relevance and effectiveness of the strategy.

Personal Space

I will try to stay in my own personal space.

Figure 3.4 Visual Cue for Personal Space

Narrative or Short Stories

Once again, a short story about personal space can be created to help clarify expectations and teach how to meet those expectations. Props such as hula-hoops or yarn can help create visual boundaries as the story is reviewed. Practice as a whole class and then refer to the story when problems arise as a way to re-teach the developing skill.

BEHAVIOR H: ROUGH PLAY

Fry (2005) has outlined that in appropriate rough play, children's faces are free and easy, their muscle tone is relaxed, and they are usually smiling and laughing. In real fighting, the facial movements are rigid, controlled, stressed, and the jaw is usually clenched.

The challenge is to help children understand how to play freely within safe boundaries.

Classroom Organization

Curtis and Carter (2005) have noted that the learning environment should provide rich opportunities for children to use their bodies both indoors and outdoors. When planning for big, rough, vigorous body play, give keen, thoughtful attention to potential safety hazards. Children need to play vigorously with their bodies, but they should do so in a safe setting. Some teachers find it helpful to draw or mark off a particular section of the room and dedicate it to big body or large muscle type play. One teacher established a "climbing zone" in her classroom by placing mats and tumble forms for safe climbing and jumping.

T-Chart

A T-Chart can be used once again to help clarify expectations. In this situation, the categories on the T-chart would be to clarify types of play that are safe and unsafe. As a class, discuss what would be examples of safe play and then what would be examples of unsafe play. Using pictures of each example can enhance the effectiveness of this strategy, especially for younger children.

Visual Cues

In addition, pictures of safe playing and/or ground rules should be posted to provide further support. For safe play with equipment, the rules may state that the slide can be used for climbing on alternate days with sliding, or that a child can climb up only after checking to make sure no one is sliding down, and that jumping can be from stationary structures only and never from swings. Other rules may say that tumbling indoors always requires a mat and cannot be done on a bare floor, and that children may only roll down hills that are fenced or away from streets and traffic. Personal visual reminders may be created for students who continue to struggle to remember the rules.

Video Modeling

Watching videos of appropriate play may be another effective teaching strategy.

Burdette and Whitaker (2005) state that when children successfully participate in big body play, it is "a measure of the children's social wellbeing and is marked by the ability of children to...cooperate, to lead, and to follow." These abilities don't just support big body play; these skills are necessary for lifelong success in relationships.

BEHAVIOR I: SCREAMING

Sometimes children are not aware that their voice has elevated to the screaming level. Screaming may occur for various reasons, including the following:

- communicating pain

- communicating frustration

- communicating fear

- communicating a need for attention

- communicating a sense of desperation.

The common thread for screaming is communication. So, adults should interpret the reason for the screaming as best as possible and respond accordingly.

Emotion Scripts

We often tell children to use their words or talk calmly when they start to scream or cry out. However, when they are frustrated or overwhelmed, their words may be hard to access and generate thoughtfully. Emotion scripts may help to communicate in more effective ways. An emotion script may have certain pictures of emotions outlined with stems or opening statements. Some examples of emotion scripts might be:

- "I feel angry because..."

- "I am worried because..."

- "I am frustrated because..."

- "I am sad because..."

The students are encouraged to point to the emotion that best describes their feeling and then fill in the speech bubble with words or pictures as further explanation. It can be very enlightening to see what is behind their emotions. This can also serve to further build the relationship between the adult and child.

Levels of Talking Chart

There are several things to consider when helping children keep their voice at an appropriate level. Teachers and parents can model in their own calm voice how they would like to be spoken to. You may even give it some clarity by connecting it to a levels chart by saying, "I am at a level 1 and I hope you can come down to a level 2 or 1 so we can both hear each other."

Using the levels of talking chart on a regular basis throughout the day becomes an effective tool to provide feedback ("You are at a 4 right now") and teach self-regulation ("Let's try to bring the voice level back to a 2 or 3. Which level can you make it to?").

Narrative or Short Story

As stated previously, a narrative or short story can be used to teach almost any skill or behavior. A story about how to use the levels of talking chart can further increase student understanding and build toward more positive behaviors.

As an example, imagine this story with photos of the children embedded:

Using an Inside Voice

It is OK to have a loud voice when I am outside.
Sometimes, I get excited when I am in the classroom.
When I get excited, I start to talk loudly.
I don't want to hurt my friend's ears in the classroom,
Or distract them from their activity.
So, I will try my best to use an inside voice in the classroom.
An inside voice means staying at a level 1, 2, or 3.

A level 4 is OK outside. I will try to save my excited voice for outside times.
I can do this!

BEHAVIOR J: AGGRESSION!

Aggression can take on many forms that can occur one at a time or in a combination of any of the following:

- biting

- kicking

- scratching

- pinching

- pushing

- pulling hair.

No single pathway is sufficient to explain the development of aggressive behavior, nor is there a single prototype of an aggressive preschooler. Research findings reveal that the critical window for intervention should be in early years. (Tremblay *et al.* 2004)

The child who lashes out often feels sad, frightened, or alone. They don't look frightened when they are about to bite, push, or hit, but fears are most likely at the heart of the problem. Fear and emotions can rob a child of their ability to think rationally and calmly.

Parents and teachers do have the ability to help a child engaging in aggressive behaviors through preventive strategies and responsive intervention techniques. In the moment, a child's aggression cannot be addressed by reasoning, punishment, or enforcing "logical consequences." The mix of intense feelings inside the child is not motivated by rewards or punishment in that moment. Once a child's behavior is out of their control, it is the responsibility of the adults around them to stay as calm as possible and do everything to help the child regain their composure.

Label Actions/Emotions

While the first course is prevention, there may be situations of aggression that arise in spite of all the best efforts. During intervention, adults always remain calm and refrain from casting blame or fault. These comments can further isolate children, and possibly exacerbate the situation. Labeling actions and feelings without judgement can be an entry into the de-escalation process once the safety of all is secured. Statements that label actions and/or feelings might include:

- "You look very upset right now. Let's take a deep breath together."

- "You are screaming very loudly and I can't understand what you need. Let's try saying that again more slowly."

- "You look very angry. Let's use a chill pass right now."

- "It looks like there is a big problem. Let's set a timer and take a minute's break so we can try to solve this problem safely."

Feelings Chart: Teach an Alternative Response

Anger and frustration are real emotions that everyone experiences to varying degrees. It is how those emotions are handled that indicates the ability to self-regulate in positive and effective ways. Children often lack those self-regulation abilities early in life and need guidance and support to develop these lifelong coping strategies.

"When you feel _____, that is very real. What are some other ways to show those feelings that are kind and gentle?"

This is a conversation that needs to happen when everyone is calm and rational. By writing or drawing pictures of healthy responses, adults can help build a menu of options of what to say and do. These options can then be organized on a problem-solving wheel or a feelings chart as in Figure 3.5.

Feelings Chart

	How I feel	What I can do
5	I need some help!	Make a cartoon Talk with someone
4	I'm really upset.	Color Think about the ocean
3	I've got a problem.	Listen to music
2	Things are pretty good.	Breathe Get a drink of water
1	Feeling great!	Take a walk

Figure 3.5 Feelings Chart

When using a feelings chart to teach alternative ways to dealing with anger or frustration, it is important to help children have a realization of their own internal signs of escalation. Consistent and thoughtful implementation of this strategy can both prevent the escalation of problem behaviors and de-escalate a situation once it has occurred. A key feature to this, and almost any other strategy, is to teach and review it when the individual is calm and there is no problem occurring at the moment. These conditions help to ensure that the brain is at its best, with most rational thinking, and that the strategy is not associated with a negative or difficult situation.

If a student can express their inner feelings, then adults could help them prevent further escalation by engaging in conversation about the problem or a calming activity. Often, however, the student has difficulty expressing those feelings until it is too late. A feelings chart may be an effective visual support to help students express how they are feeling with or without using any words.

In order for the feelings chart to be an effective strategy, students must understand the meaning of different feelings represented at each level. What does it mean to feel great versus having a problem? Connecting meaning for each feeling may require direct instruction for some students. Lessons to build this understanding can be done in a variety of ways, including the use of props or pictures of self or others. The teacher can start out the lesson by describing a certain feeling or emotion through pictures, scenarios and even video clips. This lesson includes the students participating by answering questions or acting out the different scenarios themselves. Then, the teacher can assess their understanding by asking them to toss the bean bag into the correct basket for each picture, scenario or video. Once the students understand the meaning behind the different feelings, then they are able to use the feelings chart more effectively.

The start of the day is usually a good time to use the feelings chart as the person checks in to the school routine. Unless there has been a morning problem at home or on the bus, this is usually a time where there is a clean slate from which to build. Depending on the grade level, the feelings chart may be posted as a large visual guide of feelings, or as a personal tool in a notebook, or both. The calming activities may be reviewed along with some role-playing. By using the feelings chart first thing in the morning, the teacher can assess where the students are in their feelings and respond accordingly. Responses may include celebrating and reinforcing positive feelings and offering support to those who indicate a problem is developing.

Throughout the day, look for opportunities to use the feelings chart to check in and prevent possible difficulties. My experience has been that on a scale of 1–5 (with 1 being very calm and happy), once a student has escalated to a 4 or a 5, it becomes much more difficult to de-escalate. Therefore, it is critical to intervene when students are at a 3 in order to increase the likelihood that they will be able to calm down.

Include calming activities based on student strengths, needs and interests. The following may be included as calming strategies either on the problem-solving wheel or the feelings chart:

- *Yoga cube:* "Everyone knows that if you see a shooting star, you make a wish. Ready? Sit with legs crossed. Bring palms together across your heart with fingers pointing up. Gently press hands against each other and straighten back. Inhale and bring hands over head. Exhale and lower hands to sides, twinkling your fingers. Whisper the word 'wish' as you lower your arms. As we've just seen a shooting star let's all wish for...(e.g. world peace)."

  A yoga cube can include any pose that has been taught to the students. By rolling the cube, the child can make a decision about how to calm down when it is difficult to do so when asked.

- *Sensory basket:* A sensory basket may include fidgets, play-doh, Rubik's cube, yarn, blocks, etc.

- *Breathing techniques:* An endless breathing chart or other cues for breathing can be posted. Some examples of breathing cues can be flower breathing (act like you are blowing petals off a flower), rainbow breathing (move your arms up and out as if you are blowing up a rainbow), balloon breathing (start with your hands at your mouth and then spread them out as if you are blowing up a balloon), candle breathing (act like you are blowing out candles on a cake), etc.

The feelings chart may also be used to debrief the day at the end of school. The chart may facilitate a conversation about what worked, what did not and how to make a better plan for the next day. And remember to refer to the feelings chart when the student is calm and happy. The more we celebrate those moments, the more we focus on good times and positive energy.

Real-Life Example of the Feelings Chart

As I entered a classroom for the first time, the teacher told me that one of the students was getting upset and was not sure what to do at that point. Although I had never met this student, I relied on the clarity of visual supports to assess the situation and determine the next best steps. I opened my computer and showed the student the feelings chart and explained each level briefly. Then I asked the student to tell me which level best described how he was feeling. On the scale from 1 to 5, with 5 being the most frustrated, his exact words were "I'm at a 4 and I don't know what to do about it." Although the student had not been screaming or hitting or throwing things, he felt internally that he was at a 4, a very high level of frustration.

In this example, you can see that the feelings chart not only helps students to communicate their feelings, but more importantly to determine how to calm down or de-escalate. Even in this heightened state, this student was able to identify some strategies that would be calming to him. We wrote a few strategies in the boxes to the right of the feelings column, including reading a book about planets, holding a fidget, and getting a drink of water. The feelings chart became a tool for communicating feelings and a tool for dealing with those feelings appropriately.

Chill Zone

Do you have a place in your life that you retreat to when you are feeling the stressors of the world come down on you? For some, it might be as simple as your home. For others, it might be in a specific location such as sitting on a bench in the garden or soaking in the bath tub with some soothing bubbles and lit lavender candles. Wherever your "chill zone" is, you are rejuvenated when you emerge and are better equipped to deal with the next stressful challenges that are sure to come. After all, life and stress go hand in hand. It is how a person deals with that stress that contributes to their success each day. Therefore, the "chill zone" can serve as an effective coping mechanism that promotes self-regulation.

Some may need more overt planning to identify an effective "chill zone" and an effective strategy on how to access that location and when. Knowing their own triggers can help children know when to access the "chill zone." In school settings, this may be in a pre-arranged area within a classroom or even a specific room, office, or other safe spot on the campus. As with most strategies, the "chill zone" can be more effective if there are calming elements available once they are there. When possible, decorate the "chill zone" with student interests to increase the positive feel to this area. Remember that the "chill zone" is a positive preventive strategy and not a location for a punitive time out. One young student who needed a "chill zone" had an interest in Monster Trucks. Blue Thunder was her favorite, so we found a large box and painted the wheels, doors, lights, and windshield so that she could get inside Blue Thunder to retreat, calm down, and then emerge with a positive outcome. That is the purpose of the "chill zone," after all.

Chill Passes

Data on students will help to make decisions about how many chill passes are provided for each day or portion of the day. For instance, if an individual is having difficult moments five times a day, then the teacher might provide six or seven chill passes to the student to ensure success. Over time, the data should help make ongoing decisions about how many chill passes are necessary for success. As much as possible, include the student in making these decisions.

Another feature that you may add to the chill pass is that of different times. Some chill passes might indicate that the time in the chill zone is limited to 3 minutes, while others might indicate longer times of 5, 10, or even 15 minutes. By providing different amounts of time on the chill pass, the student can make choices about how to best self-regulate their emotions and the coping strategy itself.

Literature

When having story time with your students, try to incorporate situations in which the main characters get frustrated. Work together with your students to decide how the characters in your story will respond to various negative situations. For example, if the main character is mad at their friend, you can suggest that this character takes a few deep breaths before taking any action. This will help children learn to take others' perspectives and to think about how to react in various difficult situations. You could also read stories specifically written to help with the exploration of children's negative emotions:

- *Anh's Anger* by Gail Silver. Age range: 4+.

- *When Sophie Gets Angry—Really, Really Angry* by Molly Bang. Age range: 3–7.

- *Hands Are Not For Hitting* by Martine Agassi. Age range: 2–8.

- *Teeth Are Not for Biting* by Elizabeth Verdick. Age range: 2–5.

Once the child has resumed a complete feeling of calm, then the teacher or parent can debrief the situation in an objective and rational way. In addition to reviewing what happened verbally, it is often beneficial to use some kind of visual tool to help have this conversation. This will increase the clarity of details and also keep the story objective as it is being told collaboratively and on paper. The process can unfold through a story grid or graphic organizer or a comic strip format. The use of pictures/drawings and speech bubbles helps to re-tell the situation as factually as possible. The child's perspective is heard in addition to that of the adult.

The most important part of the process then focuses on the point where a poor or unsafe behavior took place. Draw a line or arrow indicating that this was where the problem caused someone to get hurt, either physically or emotionally. Now, draw or write out several possible alternatives for a more positive and safe response. This becomes the child's plan for a better response next time, building positive momentum for positive behaviors.

Summary

Thompson (2001) states that self-confidence, relationship skills, self-management, and emotional and attentional self-regulation are among the social-emotional competencies necessary for successful participation in group learning situations.

Moreover, Kaiser *et al.* (2000) found that preschool children with deficits in these critical social skills and those who exhibit challenging behavior are more likely to have language deficits than do their typically developing peers.

Helping children to regulate their emotions doesn't necessarily happen overnight. Science tells us that the parts of the human brain that are critical to handling emotions continue to develop into adulthood. When given the right tools and supports by teachers and parents, young children can take important steps toward learning how to regulate their feelings in the face of challenging situations...a lifelong skill.

BEHAVIOR K: DIFFICULTY FOLLOWING DIRECTIONS

Listening is the core ingredient in a child's ability to follow directions. However, there are many parts to the listening process. The child not only has to hear what is being said (auditory acuity and perception), they also have to understand the meaning of the sounds and words (auditory comprehension) and interpret them into a sequence of events they must then actuate. When considering the complexities of listening, it's no wonder children struggle to follow our directions.

Positive Feedback

Teach children how to follow directions by building momentum with positive responses to preferred or fun activities. Children may be more eager to follow the direction of "cleaning up" if they have a novel job in the process. Children may be more eager to follow the direction of "staying in line" if they have a fun way to do so.

Be sure to follow with specific feedback that will provide positive reinforcement for following directions.

Positive Behavior Flip Book

A classroom where children are actively learning means there is a lot happening in many different ways. Teachers want children engaged and interacting with each other and this means that children might need help to focus on directions when given. In addition to attention grabbers, which is an auditory cue, a positive behavior flip book can provide additional support through a visual cue. With the pairing of both modalities, children can be more responsive and successful in following directions. Include pictures of your most common directives and you will always have a quick and handy tool to guide children toward building positive momentum toward this positive behavior.

Jobs and Responsibilities

Jobs and responsibilities can build on a child's need for attention and feeling successful. Create jobs that can be assigned daily, weekly or even randomly. For example, a particular student is especially struggling with following directions. Rather than give a directive that may be one more not followed, give a directive that is positive and empowering: "Jordan, you are the 'Brain Break Caller' today. Which brain break would you like to choose for the class? The monkey dance, the crazy kangaroo, or the superstar slide?"

Other fun jobs that build positive momentum toward following directions include:

- classroom greeter

- assistant teacher

- water bottle manager

- door holder

- light helper

- plant care manager

- librarian

- backpack buddy

- reporter

- star student

- pet helper

- photographer

- levels of talking manager.

Narratives or Stories to Teach Directions

Carol Gray (1994), the developer of the world-renowned, evidence-based Social Stories™ teaching strategy, outlines what is unique about this specific type of narrative. Gray states that a Social Story™ describes a situation, skill, or concept in terms of relevant social cues, perspectives, and common responses in a specifically defined style and format. The goal of a Social Story™ is to share accurate social information in a patient and reassuring manner that is easily understood by its audience. She continues to remind teachers and parents that half of all Social Stories™ developed should affirm something that an individual does well. Although the goal of a Social Story™ should never be to change the individual's behavior, that individual's improved understanding of events and expectations may lead to more effective responses.

Gray has written many wonderful books further clarifying the development and implementation of this very specific strategy, which I highly recommend. In striving to write narratives that adhere to her guidelines as much as is possible, I have found certain elements to be extremely effective:

- Incorporate photos of the children themselves in the narrative. When relevant, include photos of family members, always acquiring permission first.

- Focus on the desired behaviors without drawing attention to the problem behaviors. Those problems do not need any more highlighting and may even inadvertently serve as reminders of undesired responses.

- Provide choices of possible ways to deal with a situation or complete a task.

- Be sure to review the narrative during calm and pleasant times so that they can be useful as a form of prevention.

- Include a rationale about why the desired behavior or skill is important.

- Review prior to a situation where the child is sure to need the skill or reminders outlined in the narrative.

- Connect with children's interests when possible.

- Make the narrative fun and be positive throughout.

- At the end of the day, the narrative may be read in order to debrief how the child did that day. Self-evaluation can be a powerful reinforcer for building positive momentum.

Power Cards

Another pioneer in the world of social skill development is Elisa Gagnon, who has written about a specific type of narrative called "power cards." A power card is a brief scenario or character sketch describing how the hero solves the problem. The power card then recaps how the person working through a problem can use the same strategy to solve a similar problem.

I am often asked what the difference is between a power card and other types of narratives. While there are many similarities, I would describe their differences by saying that a power card is usually very brief and always incorporates a student's interest within the narrative. As an example, this power card helps a student to transition from a highly preferred activity to a less preferred activity using one of his favorite characters, Curious George.

POWER CARD EXAMPLE

Curious George loves to fly a kite. Sometimes, he has to stop flying a kite and do some work. Curious George wants to keep flying his kite, but he knows that he will have another chance to fly his kite later.

When it is time to stop flying a kite, Curious George will try to:

- Stop and say, "That's OK."

- Ask for one more minute.

- Ask for two more minutes.

I will try to be like Curious George and stop working on the computer when it is time to do something else.

The power card may be decorated with illustrations of the favorite character or any other positive feature, such as the student performing the desired behavior(s). As with most strategies, review the power card during calm times so that it can be effective when more stressful times occur. For another student with an interest in pirates, this power card proved highly successful after doing some research online about pirates and their code.

POWER CARD EXAMPLE: LIFE OF A PIRATE

Pirates are seen as outcasts, lawlessly sailing seas. Yet, research shows pirates made a code, rules, laws, or articles. These guidelines are shown in pirate films such as *Pirates of the Caribbean*. Let's look at some of the articles of their code.

- ARTICLE 1—None shall strike another on board the ship.

- ARTICLE 2—Each man will take care of his mate with good deeds and words.

- ARTICLE 3—Each man will do his share of work so that the ship can stay on course.

Power cards may be developed to teach almost any behavior and address most situations. The key to a power card being effective is that the brief narrative uses a preferred character or interest of the student as the central figure.

Using power cards to teach children how to follow directions can focus on those areas that the student struggles with the most. A power card to promote following directions might read as follows:

Wall-E is a great worker and does his best to listen to his boss. I will do my best and try to listen to my teachers. I will try to listen and follow these directions:

- Walk quietly in the hallways.

- Stay with my class.

- Touch others gently.

I can do this just like Wall-E!

A power card can also help deal with stressful situations, as you will see in Figure 3.6. The power card can include additional strategies such as breathing charts on the back for quick and easy access.

Being Late Is OK

Most of the time, buses run on time. It feels good when I am on time, just like the buses.

Sometimes, things happen to make us not be on time. Busy traffic or a broken motor might make a bus be late. That is OK.

Sometimes, things at school might make us not be on time or be late. If this happens, I can:

☐ Use my breathing cart

☐ Hold my surprise card

☐ Flip through my books

Remember, running late is OK. This happens to everyone. Time can be flexible and so can I.

Figure 3.6 Power Card

I once worked with a very positive and creative teacher who decided to have each child in her class write their own power card. Recognizing that we all have something we can get better at, she presented the strategy to the children, taught them how to write one and then gave them time to work either in groups or by themselves to write and decorate their power cards. When children participate in the development of strategies, they are more meaningful and effective when needed. The following power card helped a particular student with a real problem.

Mario and Luigi work well together. They are good friends and want to give other students a chance to answer questions. They might have the right answer too and this will make them feel happy. When the teacher calls on someone else in class, Mario and Luigi want you to remember that you can do one of these things:

- Wait and listen to their idea.

- Take one or two deep breaths.

- Write your answer down on a wipe off board.

At the end of the day, the class can reflect on their power card goal and self-evaluate as a way to provide positive reinforcement and specific feedback for building positive momentum toward positive behaviors.

I will create a power card to support the development of the following behavior/skill:

My power card to develop…

BUT THAT'S NOT FAIR!

Equality: the quality or state of being equal; the quality or state of having the same rights, social status, etc.

Equity: fairness or justice in the way people are treated.

So, What's the Difference?

Equal is when things are exactly alike, whereas *fair* is when decisions are made based on individual needs.

Home Example

It is equal to put all the kids to bed at the same time, and fair when parents decide on bedtime based on the age and activity level of the child.

School Example

It is equal to have all the students sit on the carpet at circle time, and fair when the teacher gives a chair to one or two students who need that to stay focused and learn.

In most case, adults anticipate the "unfair" comment more often than children actually express this kind of thinking and feeling. And when they do, adults have an opportunity to teach the lifelong lesson of fair not always meaning equal or the same.

Possible teacher responses:

- "I can see how you might feel that, but I am making sure that everyone gets what they need to learn in our classroom."

- "Let's read a story about how you're feeling and then we will talk more about it."

- "Yes, my job is to make sure that everyone gets what they need at school and that might not always feel fair. Please let me know if there is something that you need and I will do my best."

Chapter 4

CHILDREN WITH SPECIAL NEEDS

Challenges often overshadow strengths. Keep a light shining brightly on those strengths and keep the momentum moving forward.

In the US Individuals with Disabilities Education Act (IDEA), *least restrictive environment* (LRE) means that a student who has a disability should have the opportunity to be educated with non-disabled peers, to the greatest extent appropriate:

> to the maximum extent appropriate, children with disabilities, including children in public or private institutions or other care facilities, are educated with children who are not disabled, and special classes, separate schooling, or other removal of children with disabilities from the regular educational environment occurs only when the nature or severity of the disability of a child is such that education in regular classes with the use of supplementary aids and services cannot be achieved satisfactorily. (Sec. 612 (a)[5], IDEA, US Department of Education 2010)

CHARACTERISTICS OF STUDENTS WITH SPECIAL NEEDS

In the field of special education, there are different types of disabilities that will qualify a child for special services. A child may be identified as having an emotional disability, or have an autism spectrum disorder, have a medical limitation or other such need.

Moreover, these difficulties are often derived from a neurological basis. The brain can be wired differently in ways that impact auditory, visual, and sensory processing.

Autism is a complex developmental disability that typically appears during the first three years of life and is the result of a neurological disorder that affects the normal functioning of the brain, impacting development in the areas of verbal and nonverbal communication, social interaction, and the presence of repetitive behaviors or interests.

Both children and adults with autism typically show difficulties in verbal and nonverbal communication, social interactions, and leisure or play activities.

Attention-Deficit/Hyperactivity Disorder (AD/HD) is also a neurobiological disorder. Typically, children with AD/HD have developmentally inappropriate behavior, including poor attention skills, impulsivity, and hyperactivity. These characteristics arise in early childhood, typically before age seven, are chronic, and last at least six months. Children with AD/HD may also experience problems in the areas of social skills and self-esteem.

Emotional Disturbance is a condition exhibiting one or more of the following characteristics over a long period of time and to a marked degree that adversely affects a child's educational performance in the following ways:

- an inability to learn that cannot be explained by intellectual, sensory or health factors

- an inability to build or maintain satisfactory interpersonal relationships with peers and teachers

- inappropriate types of behavior or feelings under normal circumstances

- a general pervasive mood of unhappiness or depression; or

- a tendency to develop physical symptoms or fears associated with personal or school problems.

The term includes schizophrenia.

For children with an identified disability, the following characteristics are found to be common:

- difficulty processing information
- difficulty in focus and attention
- difficulty in expressing wants, needs, feelings
- difficulty in interacting with peers
- difficulty in following directions
- difficulty in understanding abstract concepts.

While these difficulties are real and need to be addressed and supported, there are also strengths to be celebrated. Children with special needs often have any or all of the following strengths:

- resilience
- intelligence
- honesty
- artistic
- musical
- humor
- perceptive
- kindness
- generosity
- tolerance.

Always remember that children with special needs are children first. They may also happen to need a bit more support or something a bit different from their friends, families, and teachers. Keep the light shining brightly on strengths and interests.

DECREASE STRESS AND INCREASE SUCCESS

Due to the neurological differences present in many children with special needs, there is often more stress as a result of these differences. Too much incoming stimuli and different wiring can make simpler tasks much more challenging. Stress can interfere with the ability to focus and perform optimally and should be minimized as much as possible. The following components all work to decrease stress in educational settings:

- Create physical and organizational structure.

- Break information down into smaller chunks.

- Present the information in a visual format.

- Incorporate an interest when possible.

- Meet sensory needs.

The form in Table 4.1 will help to describe the target behavior and antecedents and then develop a proactive plan for prevention.

⬇ Table 4.1 Plan for Prevention

Student _____ Grade _____

Teacher(s) _____ Date _____

Target Behavior:	Frequency: Duration: Intensity (1–5):
Antecedents:	
Student Strengths: Student Needs: Interests:	

Classroom Organization/ Structure	Positive Behavioral Supports: Visual Strategies and Social Skills Instruction
Sensory	
Instructional Supports	Communication Supports

Prevention: Incorporate Student Interests

Interests can increase focus, attention, and motivation. For individuals with special needs, the interests they have may even serve to decrease stress and anxiety. Almost any interest that a person has can be incorporated within a specific visual tool or behavioral strategy. By doing so, the likelihood that the tool or strategy will be effective when it is needed is increased.

One way to incorporate an interest is to simply decorate a strategy with a picture of the interest. You can put a picture of a bird, or Batman, or even a sports figure in the corner of a breathing chart and the student may be more likely to use and follow that strategy when it is time to calm down. I have seen a small decoration of an interest help a student use their schedule more successfully. By sprinkling interests across different visual strategies, the student does not have to wait for a specific time to experience that interest. This can help with the intense preoccupation with that interest and the ability to transition away from this preferred time to less preferred activities.

As an example, a student with multiple strategies had a great love for dinosaurs. The teacher was very creative in all the ways that she incorporated dinosaurs throughout these strategies in addition to specific dinosaur time...five minutes at the end of each subject area with a box of miniature dinosaurs. The teacher set a timer for five minutes to indicate how long the student could play with the dinosaurs. He also had a picture of a dinosaur on his transition marker, on his surprise card, and on his "chill pass." She added dinosaur books to the library and allowed him to write about dinosaurs in his journal every day as part of the writing activities. Before sprinkling interests throughout the strategies, the student was very resistant to following directions or completing any assignments. Once his day was dinosaur-friendly, he was successful in all academic areas. An added and unplanned result was that he started to ask for less "dinosaur time" at the end of each subject area. Perhaps the more that dinosaurs were sprinkled throughout his day, the less he felt a need to hold on so tightly.

Prevention: Classroom Organization

Classroom organization and structure is essential to a positive learning environment. This is true for all students, and especially so for students with special needs. The clearly defined and labeled areas that we discussed earlier still need to be in place in a general education or a special education setting. However, there may need to be some additional layers for students with special needs. For instance, some students may benefit from an area that is highly structured for independent work—a very separate area with very clear boundaries and labels that set a student up for success.

A student may also be more successful if there is an added layer of information to help them know how much work they need to do while in this area and what they have to look forward to upon completion. This added layer of information is often referred to as a work system, and has the same components as a mini-schedule or mini-map. A work system represents the amount and sequence of activities expected to be completed. The work system will also include what will happen when the activities are completed. This may be a reinforcing activity, the next thing on the schedule, or a transition marker that will take the child back to the schedule.

In other words, a work system accomplishes the same goals as a mini-schedule or mini-map by breaking down a section from the schedule into smaller steps or chunks which often feel more doable, increasing student willingness to engage in academic tasks.

As an example of the critical role of the classroom organization, creating clear physical boundaries in the environment can help a student self-regulate their own behaviors within each of those environments. Think of how your behavior changes from work to home, from shopping at a store to driving in your car. The environment itself guides your behavior based on the varying expectations within each of those environments. Think of this same principle and apply it to each area within a classroom. That is why having a clearly defined break area may be extremely beneficial to help transition between work and break activities more successfully. For one student who had a sensory need for roaming throughout the room for a large part of the day, the teacher created a clearly defined break with low shelves and a carpet and put down outlines of feet around the perimeter of the break area to indicate more clearly that walking or "roaming" was appropriate in the break area. The student quickly learned to self-regulate by walking in the break area and sitting in the instructional areas throughout the class. For yet another student with a sensory need for playing with water, an area was created to help meet that sensory need. By defining and labeling that area specifically for water play, the student learned to limit his water play activities to this specific area. The classroom organization can be a powerful tool for prevention for almost any behavior.

Prevention: Individual Schedules

Visual schedules are an environment support to accommodate the need for predictability and decreased anxiety about the unknown. Visual schedules take an abstract concept, such as time, and present it in a more concrete and manageable form using words and/or pictures or even objects. Schedules serve two major purposes:

- decrease stress by breaking time and/or activities into smaller chunks

- increase focus by clarifying different types of activities with varying levels of expectations

- increase motivation by clarifying when preferred activities will occur

- increase flexibility by anticipating and responding to changes more positively.

Individual schedules provide children with an understanding of what has been accomplished, what is to come, and when good things are coming. This knowledge empowers an individual to have a sense of understanding and security that leads to success and independence.

The centerpiece or core strategy of all related strategies is the visual schedule. Having established that a schedule is an essential tool for individuals with special needs, the challenge is to create a schedule that is tailored to the needs, strengths, and interests of the child. The first consideration when developing a schedule is the format. What information will the student be able to understand?

- Objects are the most concrete form and may include real objects or representational/miniature objects.

- Pictures and photographs are the next level of representation.

- Graphic symbols are somewhat more complex and consist of pictographs and written language.

- Combinations of any of the previous methods may be used to enhance student understanding.

The ability to follow written/pictorial directions is an important strength for individuals with special needs because it means that with the proper supports, the student need not be under that constant verbal direction of teachers, but can perform more independently.

Once the format is determined, then decisions must also be made regarding the schedule's location and size. Some students will need larger pictures, objects and/or words while others are successful with smaller images and representations. The schedule might be fixed on a wall, on a shelf, or in a notebook, becoming more portable. When possible, choose a location that is visually sparse and neutral, away from other areas of activity.

The individual schedule should represent the larger chunks of time throughout any given day. For instance, the schedule may include pictures, objects, or words indicating that first a student will go to homeroom, then to math, reading, lunch, PE, art, science, and then get on the bus to go home. Once they arrive at math class, there may be a more detailed breakdown of the activities that will take place for that class. This is often referred to as a "mini-schedule" or "mini-map." The amount of larger chunks reflected on the schedule may also vary from individual to individual. Some children with special needs may find it calming to know what to expect for the entire day, while others might be overwhelmed by all this information. A schedule may expose as little as one or two of the next parts of the day when necessary.

The concept of "finished" is an integral component of a schedule. Anyone who has ever compiled and used a "To Do List" understands the joy and sense of accomplishment felt when crossing off finished tasks. Therefore, the element of "finished" or closure must be incorporated into schedules developed for individuals with autism spectrum disorders. This can be accomplished in a myriad of ways, ranging from a simple check mark to placing the picture or object in a finished box or envelope. The important thing about choosing the method of indicating "finished" is like that of all other components, that it be meaningful for the student. The best way to determine whether or not you have chosen an effective means, or need to adjust it somewhat, is through trial and error.

An added layer of visual information that some students may benefit from is a link between the schedule and correlating location. This link helps the student to understand where they are to go once they have "read" their schedule by having a matching picture/icon/object/word in the location that they are to proceed to. In many cases, a basket or a pocket with a matching picture/icon/object/word may be used as a receptacle for the schedule piece.

The next consideration is that of transitioning to the schedule. How will the individual know when it is time to check their schedule? This can be done with a verbal reminder or the use of a transition marker to signal that it is time to "check your schedule," leading to future independence. Transition markers can be from something as simple as a colored card to something more complex reflecting a student's interest. Transition markers are especially effective for students who might be resistant to checking their schedule. While an individual might not be inclined to check their schedule, the power of a visual tool versus an auditory request can be very compelling. Incorporate a special interest of the student whenever possible as a calming mechanism, as in Figure 4.1.

Check Schedule

Figure 4.1 Check Schedule Visual Tool

Never underestimate the power of a highly focused interest. A perceptive teacher or parent will use that interest whenever possible rather than strive to stifle or control it. A particular young man comes to mind with two strong, if not overwhelming, interests: Country/Western magazines and Disney characters. When introduced to a visual schedule, he was not inclined to "check his schedule"—especially after viewing what it had to offer. Once his interests were strategically incorporated into the daily routine, his enthusiasm for checking his schedule increased dramatically. By knowing when good things were coming, he was able to follow the routine and stay focused during less interesting activities. Consistency is the key. When things are going well, there might be a tendency to function on an auditory level—that which is quickest, easiest, and most natural. But when things are not going well, then the visual schedule is used—usually not with any great success. A critical key to achieving success is to remember that all visual strategies, especially individual schedules, must be taught during calm times in order to be effective during rough seas. It is neither fair nor realistic to expect an individual with autism to respond to something that is new or inconsistent at their worst, most stressful moments.

Teach, assess, and revise. The good news is that schedules definitely help to make the world more predictable and less confusing, and by doing so can help to minimize behavioral difficulties. The bad news is that schedules almost always require revisions after implementation. In other words, educators and parents teach the visual tool through modeling, guiding, and physical assistance, and then adjust the size, location, format, and other details based on individual performance. The process of trial and error can be complex and frustrating, but is a necessary aspect of the development of a tailored and effective schedule. Educators and parents must be prepared to make changes and more changes until the visual tool is effective.

Use the planning tool in Table 4.2 to help create a tailor-made individual schedule.

Table 4.2 Planning Tool for an Individual Schedule

Student:	Teacher:	Date:
Individual Schedule Considerations:	**Plans:**	
1. Schedule Format: What does the student understand best when under stress?	☐ Actual objects (e.g. cup that can be used for drinking) ☐ Representative objects (e.g. miniature bus for going home) ☐ Partial objects (e.g. bubble wand for break time) ☐ Photographs ☐ Clip Art—B&W ☐ Clip Art—color ☐ Line Drawings ☐ Words ☐ Combination of any of these formats ☐ Other: _____	
2. Schedule Location: Where will the schedule be located?	☐ Neutral wall—top to bottom ☐ Neutral wall—left to right ☐ Notebook ☐ Clipboard ☐ Computer ☐ Other: _____	

3. Schedule Content:	School	Home
What are the "big chunks" that will make up the schedule? Examples: • Breakfast • Reading • Math • Outside • Lunch • Science • PE • Choir • Bus/Home	☐ _____ ☐ _____ ☐ _____ ☐ _____ ☐ _____ ☐ _____ ☐ _____ ☐ _____ ☐ _____ ☐ _____ ☐ _____	☐ _____ ☐ _____ ☐ _____ ☐ _____ ☐ _____ ☐ _____ ☐ _____ ☐ _____ ☐ _____ ☐ _____ ☐ _____
4. Schedule Length: How much of the schedule should be displayed?	☐ Whole day ☐ Half day ☐ Part day ☐ First/then ☐ Other: _____	

Individual Schedule Considerations:		Plans:
5. Transition: How will he/she transition back to the schedule?	☐ Verbal cue ☐ Visual cue ☐ Timer/clock ☐ Transition marker ☐ Other: _____	
6. Schedule Completion: How will the student know when each part of the schedule is finished?	☐ Look at schedule and check off ☐ Look at schedule and turn icon/object around ☐ Move arrow as activities are completed ☐ Move icons from a "to do" section to an "all done" section ☐ Take icon/object from the schedule and place in a pocket at the bottom of the schedule ☐ Take icon/object from the schedule and place on a matching icon/object at destination ☐ Other: _____	
7. Individual Interests: How does the schedule incorporate the student's interests?	☐ Preferred activities are strategically placed after non-preferred ☐ Schedule is decorated with high-interest object/character ☐ Transition marker is decorated with a high-interest object/character ☐ Other: _____	

Prevention: First…Then Board

The concept of "first…then" is usually founded on the premise that one must first complete work before getting to enjoy a break or other preferred activity. The first…then board helps a student stay focused and engaged during morning circle time by seeing that center time is coming up next, which is a highly preferred activity. While the first…then board can be used for any difficulty moment, it is often a more personal version of the class schedule.

The Premack Principle states that behavior occurring at a high frequency can be used to increase the rate of behavior that occurs at a low frequency. Premack (1959) states: "For any pair of responses, the independently more probable one will reinforce the less probable one."

However, the first…then strategy may be used to help an individual get their needs met first and then be better prepared for work. Have you ever taken a nap in order to be refreshed to face a daunting task? Or have you ever eaten some of your dessert before the main course? When compromising, remember to do so *with* the strategy instead of abandoning the strategy.

Prevention: Mini-Schedule or Mini-Map

Now that we have established the core strategy of an individual schedule as an essential starting point for some students, let's extend our focus to a companion strategy. A schedule within a schedule has many names. For our purposes, we will call this sub-strategy a "mini-map." A mini-map takes a piece of the schedule and breaks it down even further. The schedule guides you from one major activity to another, while the mini-map clarifies the smaller steps within that activity. This can be especially helpful to decrease frustration associated with academic tasks, but can be useful for any chunk of time that presents a challenge. Some individuals with Asperger's have difficulty with experiences that are too sensory in one way or another. Going to PE or taking a bath/shower can be broken down into smaller steps so that an individual can walk through these difficult experiences with a guide and a clear understanding that there is an end in sight.

For now, let's focus on mini-maps as they relate to academic endeavors. Often, teachers note that a common antecedent or trigger to behavioral difficulties is the presentation of academic tasks. The behaviors can range from a verbal protest to a meltdown when students feel overwhelmed by school work. The first question to ask, of course, is what is there about the work that makes the student feel so overwhelmed? Does the page look too busy? Is too much handwriting involved? Are there too many problems? Is it too difficult or too easy? If so, then we must adjust the format and/or content of academic tasks to increase student success.

The schedule says it is time for math. The student struggles consistently with math and typically puts his head down and produces little or no work. But with a mini-map, the student feels more able to get started and move forward. The mini-map is often a small checklist and can be decorated with a student interest to increase focus and motivation. This checklist then breaks down the expectations during math into smaller chunks. The mini-map or checklist might say something like this:

1. Warm-up activity _____

2. Test review _____

3. Do problems 3–10 _____

4. Discuss with partner _____

Next: five-minute break.

This mini-map often reduces the anxiety associated with challenging academics so that the student is more likely to get started and even more likely to continue, especially if there is a motivator at the end of the work.

Real-Life Example of a Mini-Map

A kindergarten student with an autism spectrum disorder was struggling to participate successfully during Computer Lab time. The expectation for that class was to have the children complete a specific reading program called iStation. This student, however, had a different idea about how he would like to engage in reading through a different program called StarFall. The student would immediately go to his computer and eagerly open up the StarFall program. The antecedent to his behavior of screaming and throwing objects was being told to close down the program and go to iStation instead. Most of the 30 minutes that was supposed to be dedicated to the reading program was spent dealing with the disruptive behavior of this student. Considering that the student was getting no instruction on the required program, the staff agreed that at least some time positively engaged in the required program would be better than the current situation. They created a left to right mini-map with a picture of StarFall first, followed by a picture of the iStation program, and then one more picture of StarFall. At a quick glance, the student now saw that he could begin with his preferred activity and then he would do just a little bit of his less preferred activity before getting even more time on his preferred activity. The mini-map supported the student by building positive momentum toward completing desired outcomes in incremental steps.

Mini-Schedules or Mini-Maps at Home

This seemingly simple strategy of a mini-schedule or mini-map can be highly effective to address "rough spots" in different environments. Remember that a mini-map is a visual strategy that takes a chunk of time and breaks it down even further. While we have seen how this can prevent work avoidance behaviors at school, let's shift the focus to an overlapping struggle that is common at home...homework!

Many students with special needs struggle to navigate the waters of school life, only to come home and face more academic work. It is probably safe to say that most students would rather not deal with homework in the evenings. However, the difference is that the students with special needs often work harder all day long to deal with not only academic stressors but also the added challenges of social interaction and possibly sensory overload, creating a cumulative effect with different possible results.

I found myself in a situation recently and was reminded of the real and debilitating impact of this cumulative effect. I had finished a long day at work and was driving home. However, home was 150 miles away and I started my trip at 6:00 in the evening. So, I was tired and had a bit of a drive in front of me. Oh well, I had got to get home that night. Then, it started to rain heavily. I slowed down and paid more attention. Then, a caravan of big trucks started to speed past me. Now, I had to work much harder to stay in my lane and see where I was going. I noticed that I had both hands on the wheel now and was sitting straight up to see the road better. Then, a construction vehicle moved into my lane directly in front of me. The lights on this truck were not only very bright, but were flashing in a random pattern at every corner of the truck, creating a disco effect. So now, I was tired on a rainy night with my windshield wipers moving as fast as they could against this sea of bright lights. I wanted to look away, but realized this could be catastrophic on a highway. So, I took the next exit and stopped at the first gas station. Some might call this "driving avoidance," but I call it survival. I think that might be how some of our children feel.

So, at the end of a long and stressful day, a student might have to face homework. A mini-map of the evening activities may be all it takes to help them get started, knowing that their favorite activity takes place right before homework time, right after homework time, or both. And some children might benefit from a mini-map/checklist of the homework chunk of time itself. For instance, the homework mini-map might read:

1. Get your materials ready.

2. Reading assignment.

3. Math problems.

4. Review with Mom or Dad.

Next: Have fun on the computer for 30 minutes?

Mini-maps can also help with other rough spots at home. Some examples include household chores, personal hygiene routines, and shopping trips. One family found mini-maps to be helpful even for car rides. Their son would take off his seat belt repeatedly, causing many stops along the way. A mini-map was created that included pictures and words that directed him to:

1. Buckle your seatbelt.

2. Keep it buckled.

3. Listen for Mom or Dad to say it is time to unbuckle.

No more unplanned road stops for this family.

Checklists and Compromise

In this example, the checklist had been written and mapped out that the student was to watch a video about Texas, then read a Social Story about having a substitute, review the Texas map and then have time to flip through his book for break, which was positive reinforcement for this student.

However, after the video, the student asked to have his book to flip through, which was supposed to happen after he completed the three tasks. It was in the afternoon and he'd had a successful day so far and he had completed the first task on the list successfully as well. Given the entire context and because the student used his words calmly to request what he felt he needed, a desired behavior, the teacher reinforced that by honoring his request and adding five minutes of "book flipping" time before proceeding to the next activity. By adding this to the checklist, the compromise became part of the original plan now.

After the five-minute timer rang, the student stopped flipping through his book, put the book away, and resumed the next planned activity of reading the story. He successfully completed this and the map activity. He then asked if he could change his book flipping time to Google Maps time, another highly preferred activity. The teacher and the student also made this adjustment to the checklist and he successfully transitioned to the next subject on his schedule, which was PE. Some students will require more flexibility and compromise than others when implementing strategies. Remember to work compromise into the strategy so that the strategy continues to have meaning.

Prevention: T-Chart

A T-chart (see Figure 3.1) can be made by placing a line down the middle of a page and labeling the left and right side of the page according to acceptable and unacceptable behavior. The T-chart is then used to clarify acceptable or desired behaviors versus unacceptable or undesired behaviors by listing those under each of the categories. I once worked with a teacher addressing a problem with profanity. He had many conversations with the student and had already tried several other strategies, but the profanity continued to spew. I offered the T-chart as a possible strategy and the teacher immediately told me that the student knew she was not supposed to say those words, but she just didn't care about that rule. He was trying to tell me that writing appropriate words on one side of the T-chart and inappropriate words on the other side was just too simple. Perhaps a bit reluctantly, the teacher implemented the T-chart strategy over the next few days. He had incorporated the student's interest in *Pirates of the Caribbean* by placing a picture of a good pirate and a menacing pirate on each side to support the concept. In addition, he sat down with her during a calm time and asked her to come up with some new words that she could say instead of her current repertoire. She came up with very special words that she could use instead of the usual—Holy Plankton and Holy Macaroni were just a few. The teacher was surprised and pleased that this very simple strategy did, in fact, support a positive change in behavior.

T-chart considerations:

- When possible, generate both lists with the student. If student input is not possible, then collaborate with teachers and parents to identify what is most meaningful for the student.

- Pictures may enhance the effectiveness of this strategy.

- Review during calm times. The beginning of the day or each class may be good opportunities.

- Refer back to the T-chart when the targeted behavior occurs. Practice replacement behaviors from the acceptable list.

- The T-chart may incorporate a special interest, increasing the effectiveness of this strategy

- The T-chart may be posted in the class or located in a student folder/notebook.

Another variation of the T-chart strategy is to use it to clarify what a class rule "looks like" and "sounds like" as a way to increase meaning and understanding of class rules and expectations.

Prevention: Puzzle Piece Strategy

When using the puzzle piece strategy, as shown in Figure 4.2, it is recommended to begin with a clear understanding of what the student is expected to accomplish to earn each piece of the puzzle. This may be completion of a specific activity or even a specific amount of time that desired behaviors are demonstrated.

Figure 4.2 Puzzle Piece Strategy

While there may be an instance when the student does not earn the next puzzle piece when the desired behavior is not performed, the puzzle pieces should not be removed once they are earned. When implemented in this way, the strategy promotes building positive momentum toward desired behaviors.

Puzzle piece strategy:

- Insert a picture/photo of a highly desired thing or activity into the center of a blank document.

- Print out two copies of this document.

- Keep one page as is and laminate. Cut up the other page into smaller pieces as if forming a puzzle. Consider how many pieces you expect the child to need to earn to complete the puzzle (e.g. four as in Figure 4.2). Use Velcro to stabilize the pieces.

- Guide the student to place one of the puzzle pieces on the original with Velcro as they complete an assigned activity or perform desired behaviors for a specific amount of time.

- Once they complete the entire puzzle, then they are able to enjoy the highly desired thing or activity for a predetermined amount of time.

Prevention: Star Board

The star board is yet another format to provide positive reinforcement that builds positive momentum, as shown in Figure 4.3. The student is encouraged to choose their reward before beginning to work and place it at the top of the board. Then, the student earns a star for completion of specific tasks or a designated amount of time engaged in a desired behavior. Once all the stars are place on the board, then the positive reinforcement takes place, usually with a predesignated time limit.

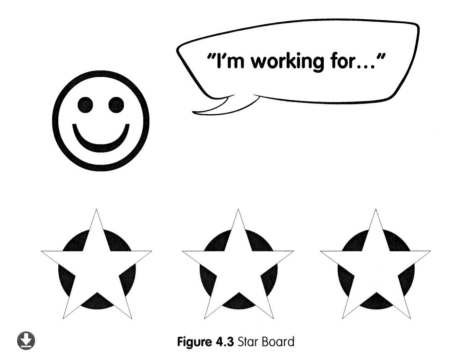

Figure 4.3 Star Board

Prevention: Flip Card Strategy

A flip card is a quick and easy visual strategy which highlights one behavior and clarifies through graphics and words when certain behaviors are acceptable and when they are not.

Place a visual that indicates that it is OK to engage in the target behavior on one side of the paper. Place a different visual that indicates it is not OK to engage in the specific behavior at this time on the other side of the paper. Think of it as a version of an "Open" and "Closed" sign in a store window. The sign, or flip card, gets turned around to indicate when it is OK to enter and when it is not. Much in the same way, the flip card will tell the student when it is OK to do a particular behavior and when it is no longer appropriate. Of course, not every behavior lends itself to this strategy. Again, it is only for behaviors that are acceptable some of the time.

As an example, a student found great pleasure in singing and talking to himself...constantly. The teaching assistant sat near the student so that he could tell him to be quiet through whispers, a shake of the head and quite a few "Shhhhs." The student would try to oblige, but his silence would only last a few seconds. The to and fro between the teaching assistant and the student became more bothersome than that actual singing and talking after a while.

I took out a piece of paper and drew two pictures on each side (in spite of an incredible lack of artistic talent). On one side of the paper I drew a universal sign for "no" and wrote "no singing or talking for now." On the other side of the paper, I drew a happy face and a speech bubble that said, "Now I can sing or talk in a low voice."

I showed him both sides and then left it on the table in front of him in plain view. He looked at the flip card, he looked at me, and then he sat there quietly for a moment. Then, it was like a light bulb came over his head. He flipped the card over to the other side and started singing again. I was so excited! He not only understood the strategy, he tried to achieve his goals by *using* the strategy. I simply turned the card back over and told him not yet. He was not happy about the directive, but he did follow the directions of the flip card. When the activity was over, I flipped the card over to indicate that he could now sing and talk to his heart's content. He did seem very content. This strategy was generalized into different settings with equal effectiveness. As with most strategies, the flip card becomes a more powerful strategy when a favorite character or interest is incorporated.

Prevention: Narratives or Stories

Narratives or stories have been discussed in the previous chapter to teach skills and positive behaviors. Once again, narratives or stories can be effective in preventing difficulties and offering positive solutions. A narrative can validate feelings, provide a solution, and even offer comfort during a stressful time.

The following is an example of a narrative written to help deal with sensory issues. This narrative was written for a student who wanted to hug her classmates frequently and deeply to get that deep pressure feeling.

BEING A GOOD FRIEND

My name is _____ and I am in the
_____ grade at _____ elementary.

I work very hard and try to listen to the teacher.

I love all different colors. My favorite color is pink.

This makes me happy.

I have good friends at school.

I can shake hands with my friends.

I can shake hands with my teachers.

I can even give a side hug if that is OK with them.

I will ask first.

I can do this!

The end...my friend.

With photos of the student, her classmates and teachers included, the story was a big hit with her and the entire class.

Prevention: Topic Card

Some students tend to perseverate on a particular topic that is of great interest to them. Topic cards can help students engage in a variety of topics, beyond their own interests, connecting with others socially. They include just a few words that describe a topic that helps to launch a student or group students in a particular direction.

A teacher had created a special lunch group to help a student with special needs engage in appropriate teen conversations. She had one main interest and it would dominate every conversation. Her interest was in princesses and everything to do with them. While the other children enjoyed talking about princesses some of the time, they grew weary of it being the topic of discussion *all* of the time. This narrow conversational topic had also narrowed her circle of friends to almost none. While the teacher had good intentions, simply creating a lunch group to help her engage in other topics had not been successful. The students needed some supports to be effective in their role as peer teachers. The teacher chose topic cards as the best strategy for this situation.

Instead of just choosing different topics from her own repertoire, the teacher recruited ideas from the typical peers. She asked them what kinds of things they liked to talk about and the first thing they said was "drama." The teacher thought they were referring to the arts, but when she asked for further explanation, they described drama as "who likes who," "who is in an argument" and "who is in trouble." You know, drama. From this conversation with the typical peers, the teacher compiled the topic cards with pictures and words. The topics included drama, the weekend, movies, games, jokes, favorite things, school work, and birthdays.

Once the topic cards were compiled, the teacher sat with them at lunch one day to teach them how to use the cards effectively. The cards were piled in the middle of the table and the students took turns as they turned the cards over, much like a game. The topic cards guided their conversation as a group and served to help the student with a special need stay focused on the topic at hand. The students should feel comfortable in referring to the cards during conversations as a positive support. By practicing the use of the topic cards in a safe setting, the students are more likely to use them in new and different situations. This lunch group became very effective in using the topic cards at lunch time and at other times throughout the day.

Prevention: Power Card

As stated in Chapter 3, power cards are brief summaries that describe a problem along with possible solutions. The power card is developed by using a student interest as the main character. The power card should be reviewed frequently to be effective as a preventive strategy. In times of difficulty, the power card may also be reviewed as an instructive consequence.

EXAMPLE: POWER CARD FOR SOLVING A PROBLEM
THE HULK SOLVES A PROBLEM

The Hulk is a super hero and is very strong.

Sometimes, the Hulk has a problem. When he has a problem, he takes a deep breath inside and makes his chest extra big. Then he says, "That's OK. I can do this."

So, when you have a problem, the Hulk wants you to remember that you can also:

- Take a deep breath.

- Make your chest extra big.

- Say, "That's OK. I can do this."

Prevention: Video Modeling

Stress and anxiety create a negative situation, which makes learning difficult. In a traditional teaching situation the need for person-to-person interaction can in and of itself be a cause of stress and anxiety. A child is unnecessarily burdened by the need to overcome this stress and anxiety before they can focus on what is being taught.

Video modeling is a strategy that helps to minimize that stress and allow the child to have full benefit of what it looks like to perform the desired skill or behavior. An important benefit of video modeling is that it removes the necessity of person-to-person interaction from the learning process. Removing this interaction takes pressure off the child and allows them to concentrate on the video. Attending to the video only, a learner concentrates and is more focused and less distracted.

Bellini and Akullian (2007) have described video modeling as a strategy involving the use of videos to provide modeling of targeted skills. Sherer *et al.* (2001) have found that both videos that include the participants (video self-modeling, VSM) and videos of others are effective in teaching new skills.

Video modeling including "other" models may be easier to produce because these videos generally require less editing than VSM; typically developing students may more readily cooperate, understand directions, already demonstrate mastery of target skills, and require fewer prompts.

The videos are short, usually two to five minutes, or possibly even shorter depending on the desired behavior or skill. The student will typically watch the video three to five times at one session. The student will then practice the skill/behavior targeted in the video. The teacher might say, "Now it's your turn, just like the video" and support the student as they attempt the skill/behavior. Continue to create opportunities to practice the new skill at natural and planned times throughout the day.

When making your own video, here are some ways to highlight important information once you have secured photo releases:

- clear and positive title

- slow motion

- up close—zoom in

- highlight single words

- use text

- use symbols

- use magnetic letters for titles

- incorporate student drawings.

One of the most important components to video modeling is that only desired behaviors are included in the final video. Any inappropriate or distracting behaviors captured during the filming of the video should be edited out, leaving only the positive and desired behaviors.

There are also pre-made videos to teach social skills and positive behaviors on YouTube and other apps. Some of the videos made available through YouTube include the following skills and behaviors:

- making friends

- taking turns

- greeting others in the hallway

- accepting "no"

- taking a break to calm down

- cafeteria skills

- walking in the hallway

- and many, many more...

Video modeling has proven to be a highly effective strategy to teach desired behaviors and skills when implemented during calm times with opportunities for practice and feedback. An additional by-product of this strategy is that it often builds the relationship between the student and the teacher, creating a more positive interaction related to behavioral shaping and building positive momentum.

Prevention: Handwriting Supports

The process of writing requires much more than the ability to form pretty letters and can often be a source of frustration. For some children, data may indicate that handwriting tasks are actually a trigger or antecedent to work avoidant behaviors. Oehler (2013) has stated that the writing process involves skills in language, organization, motor control and planning, and sensory processing—four areas that are problematic for many individuals with special needs and, in particular, students with an autism spectrum disorder. It is essential that parents and teachers consider how each of these areas may be affecting a student's aversion to the writing process and recognize it as a legitimate stressor.

There are many handwriting supports available, thanks to the broadening world of technology. Some of the tools to prevent frustration related to handwriting include the following:

- graphic organizers

- computer/portable word processor

- speech-to-text programs (e.g. Dragon Dictation)

- alternate keyboard

- low-tech writing tools

- timers to build endurance

- auditory feedback programs

- iPad apps

- handheld dictionary

- Writing with Whole Words programs.

Communication Bill of Rights: National Joint Committee (NJC) for the Communication Needs of Persons with Severe Disabilities

The NJC for the Communication Needs of Persons with Severe Disabilities has put forth a Communication Bill of Rights which emphasizes the critical nature of communication. One can take for granted the ability to request desired objects or activities, reject undesired objects or activities, or simply offer a comment on a moment. Perhaps most importantly, the Communication Bill of Rights reminds us to presume competence at all times and speak about the child as if they understand all that we are saying.

For more information, go to the NJC website.[5]

Prevention: Communication Systems

Research in the area of behavior support has repeatedly demonstrated the positive effects of learning more effective and efficient communication on the challenging behaviors of individuals with developmental disabilities.

An inability to communicate effectively can have detrimental effects from behavior to the quality of one's life. This can often lead to the following behaviors:

- frustration

- aggression

- disengagement

- dependence.

---

5   www.asha.org/njc

Unaided communication systems rely on the user's body to convey messages. Examples include gestures, body language, and/or sign language.

Aided communication systems require the use of tools or equipment in addition to the user's body. Aided communication methods can range from paper and pencil, to communication books or boards, to devices that produce voice output (speech generating devices or SGDs) and/or written output. Electronic communication aids allow the user to use picture symbols, letters, and/or words and phrases to create messages. Some devices can be programmed to produce different spoken languages.

When a child communicates through gestures or body language alone (a form of unaided communication), their behavior may be misunderstood as something other than what was intended. As an example, a student who was nonverbal and using his body to communicate was running out of the classroom on a regular basis. Staff worked to stop the behavior, but without aided communication, the reason behind the behavior was misinterpreted. The student loved playing on the swings and the staff assumed that the student was running out of the room to go out to the swings. Of course, staff would prevent the student from getting too far for safety reasons, so the behavior was redirected without fully understanding his perspective.

The team, including the teacher, parent, and speech pathologist, recognized the need for an aided communication system and created pictures of highly preferred activities and basic needs. They conducted lessons to teach the meaning and use of the pictures to communicate more effectively. After several days of teaching the student how to use the pictures, he started to run out of the classroom as he had previously. However, before any staff could intervene, the student went to his picture book and selected the "bathroom" picture and handed it to his teacher. This aided communication built a powerful bridge between the teacher and student and provided insight into the running out behavior. He had been taking care of his needs with the only tools that he had available, himself.

More recently, augmentative and alternative communication strategies have been receiving increased attention as primary teaching goals for young children limited verbal expression. The use of pictures and choice-making opportunities has been reported to facilitate language acquisition and/or result in increased communicative attempts across daily routines.

The team should assess the student's strengths, needs, and interests when determining the most appropriate aided communication system. There are many options, which range from simple low technology systems to very sophisticated high technology systems. The following are but a few examples:

- Picture Exchange

- Choice Boards

- Yes/No Boards

- Eye Gaze Boards

- Sound Board App

- Cheap Talk 8

- ProLoQuo2Go

- LAMP (Language Acquisition through Motor Planning)

- and many, many more...

When teaching how to use the communication system, whether it is low or high tech, always try to honor as many communicative attempts as possible. This will strengthen the understanding of how to communicate and will also serve to build the relationship between the adults and child. Later in the process, this may also help the child to accept a "no" better because they understand that they are being heard. Maybe next time.

There are multiple free low-technology communication resources available at the Prentke Romich Company (PRC) AAC Language Lab website.[6]

---

6   https://aaclanguagelab.com/resources/free

DEFINING A MELTDOWN

When dealing with meltdowns, the most important things to consider are the triggers that lead to a meltdown. It might appear that the behavior just erupts out of nowhere, but there is almost always a trigger. It might be a series of things that have a cumulative effect, making it difficult to ascertain just one culprit. However, good data collection that looks closely at the antecedents will provide some clues. Data on the antecedents, or triggers, should include the time of day, persons involved, specific activities and location. Any other relevant information, such as changes in medication, illness, or other physiological conditions, should be included.

Finding the trigger is the most essential component in preventing a meltdown. It is our best hope in helping an individual avoid the trigger(s) and/or develop coping mechanisms to deal specifically with that trigger. It has been said that a meltdown is like having your emotions hijacked. This is an important understanding for adults trying to understand and support a person as they struggle through this stressful and difficult experience. As one student put it after such an experience, "Meltdowns are terrible."

Once the triggers are identified, then a plan can be developed either with or for the child with special needs to deal with feelings of anger or anxiety in acceptable ways. The feelings chart that has been reviewed previously is just one strategy intended to help identify coping strategies when feelings escalate toward a meltdown.

Intervention: Checklist

When strategies are used consistently as preventive strategies, those very same strategies may be effective as an intervention to prevent further difficulties or escalation. As an example, a student was starting to have a meltdown when a school program in the cafeteria rehearsal went on a bit too long. He was escorted into the hallway to minimize the stressors, but once he was in the hallway, he repeatedly asked to return to the program. He kept saying that he needed to finish the show, finish the show, finish the show…

The student was very familiar with checklists as they were used consistently to help him be successful in his academic activities. He had several different checklists that were decorated with a variety of his highly preferred characters.

A checklist was presented and he was asked to check off the first item that indicated the show was finished. He said that it was time for PE and staff explained that today was a surprise day and that there was no PE due to the program. Again, he was asked to check off the first box on his checklist.

Once he checked it off, staff told him that it was time for a break and that he could choose to take his break outside or in class. He circled that he would like to go outside. When the timer went off, he checked off the next box on his checklist and went to class.

Upon returning to class, the checklist included highly preferred activities to promote a positive transition back to his routine (e.g. snack, magnets).

After finishing a snack and building with the magnets, he checked off his checklist and then watched science videos (to try to align with his regular schedule as much as is possible). The student completed the science videos, checked off his checklist and then had a final break before leaving for the day.

Prevention: Meeting Sensory Needs

While many people have sensory differences, children with special needs may have more prominent sensory differences that add stress and interfere with daily activities. However, there are many supports that can be put in place to minimize those sensory differences. When possible, consult with an occupational therapist to assess a child's needs and determine the most appropriate supports necessary for that child.

Auditory Sensitivity

Although the hum of the air conditioner seems like mild background noise that is easy to filter for a neuro-typical person, it might sound like a small jet flying overhead with no end for a person with a special need, especially an autism spectrum disorder. So, this is real and overwhelming and difficult to explain in ways that others can fully understand. However, it is a primary concern related to instructional and behavioral success. The following are a few ways that teachers and families can support individuals with auditory sensitivity

- Headphones and/or earplugs can offer comfort and relief for many students. Noise-canceling headphones are the most effective as they replace irritating environmental noise by producing calming white noise.

- Fans to create background or "white noise."

- Gradual introduction to noise which might happen in a few ways. Perhaps a student who has difficulty with the roar of lunch time might be allowed to enter the cafeteria before others so as to prepare for the gradual increase of noise as students enter. There might also be a designated place where they can go if it reaches an uncomfortable level. Another way might be to go to a loud grocery store for one minute and then wait outside for the remainder of the shopping trip (if safe). The time is then gradually increased as the student is able to handle the level of noise without feeling overwhelmed and/or stressed.

- Provide an alternative yet comparable setting. At school, sitting outside at lunch time might be preferable to sitting inside the cafeteria. At home, families may be selective in their choice of restaurants so as to create a relaxing dining environment.

Visual Sensitivity

Approximately 70 percent of information about the world is taken in through the eyes. First, it should be noted that research exploring the brains of individuals on the autism spectrum has found that there is generally a heightened awareness of visual details. Also, the brain processes information and makes decisions/plans in the visual region of the brain (Bertone *et al.* 2005). The sense of vision is critical for all individuals and the implications for differences in this sense is especially important to understand.

Let's start with the finding that there is a heightened awareness of visual details. I remember one student who kept trying to remove a lump of mascara from my eye because he found it very disturbing. Or the student who kept insisting that the "zero" that the teacher had drawn on the smart board was a "six" because she had put a tiny tail at the top left of the "zero." He would not move on until she drew a proper zero. Some of the implications of this difference is that a simple worksheet might look like a sea of words that never end. This is likely to be misinterpreted as work avoidance if the student refuses to complete the worksheet or read the page. Teachers and parents can help by increasing the size of the font and adding more white space on the paper. This will help to make it look less overwhelming. Although the information might need to be on two pages instead of one, the student might be able to feel as though they can be successful with this format. Another strategy might be to place each problem or paragraph on an index card so that the student only sees the necessary information at any one time. And still another is to create a window that can slide up and down a page so that the student only sees one section at a time. Other visual supports might include color coding, start and stop points, arrows, and post-it notes with guiding information.

Another possible difference with the sense of vision may be light sensitivity. Possible supports include, but are not limited to, decreased fluorescent lighting and increased natural lighting, sunglasses, caps, shades, and light coverings. You can find light covers that are safe at several occupational therapy websites.

Tactile Sensitivity

For some children, certain textures feel aversive or even painful. For these individuals, the idea of a hug or even accidentally brushing up against something may be highly stressful. In order to prevent this negative tactile experience, much energy and focus is paid to avoiding situations that increase the likelihood of such events. Imagine lining up where there are others in front of you and behind you. The chances of being accidentally touched by either person may cause the simple act of lining up to be highly stressful and anxiety provoking. For individuals who do not like the feel of certain textures or things, parents and teachers may consider the following types of supports:

- *Clothing adjustments:* Wear worn or softer clothes, remove tags, cover seams, etc.

- *Allow seating options that provide a safe barrier from others:* Sit on a bean bag or chair during large group activities; remain at desk while others sit on the floor, etc.

- *Allow lining up options:* Stand at the front or back of the line to increase control over distance from others.

And yet others with sensory differences might actually seek out certain types of touch. There are some individuals with an autism spectrum disorder who like big hugs or touching certain textures. For these individuals, occupational therapists (OTs) can help to identify activities or equipment that can help provide this sensory feedback throughout the day. With the expertise and input of an OT, weighted vests/blankets, wiggle cushions, and other materials may be recommended. Some individuals who seek out pressure find comfort in a body sock. This neat multisensory "time in" tool is excellent for providing calming/organizing, deep pressure input, and for developing motor planning, spatial, and body awareness. Body socks can be wonderful for tactile and deep pressure proprioceptive seekers, and even for those who are tactilely defensive.

Taste Differences
Many parents experience the "picky eater" from time to time. However, the difference in describing child with a special need as a picky eater can be found in the intensity or degree. Lack of understanding regarding this difference can sometimes lead to criticism of the parent.

First and foremost, is there a way to supplement the diet to ensure adequate nutrition?

For many individuals with narrow food interests, it can be very much about the texture of the food(s). While some individuals will only eat crunchy foods, others might only eat soft or blended foods. And yet others might respond mostly to the smell of the food. In addition, it may be that the need for sameness may contribute significantly to the ritualistic lunch or dinner. Only eating spaghetti for lunch day in and day out might actually be very comforting for an individual with a high stress level due to the neurological differences in autism.

Understanding the drive behind the narrow food preference may offer some insight as to how to proceed. The following are but a few ways to expand upon the food preferences.

- Offer a visual list of the meal, adding a small amount of new food on the list at a strategic place. Perhaps the list will indicate to start out with a highly preferred food item, followed by a small amount of a new food item, and then again followed by the rest of the highly preferred food and drink.

- Introduce foods that have similar qualities to the individual's current preferences, but expand slightly beyond.

- Introduce new food in small increments that will build toward success. For example, if you are trying to add healthy fruit to a diet, perhaps you will place a grape off to the side of the plate for the first few days, followed by a few days of smelling the grape, and then licking the grape and then eating a small section of the grape until the person has an increased tolerance for the grape.

- If there is a strong interest that the child finds very appealing, use that interest to help introduce new foods when possible. For instance, cut out a sandwich in the shape of an elephant or SpongeBob or any other preferred item or character.

Motor Lab or Sensory Room

Cohen *et al.* (2006) have found that children's sensory processing problems have a strong relationship to their behavior difficulties. Many schools have found great benefit in dedicating a specific room to meet the diverse sensory needs of their students. By meeting those needs, they often see a decrease in behaviors that stem from sensory differences, at least in part. A motor lab or sensory room is a specific room with specific sensory equipment and activities selected to benefit specific sensory processing needs.

General suggestions when developing a motor lab or sensory room include the following:

1. Consult with an OT whenever possible.

2. Assess the needs of the students.

3. Structure the sensory experiences as stations or centers using labels, mini-schedules and/or choice boards.

4. Develop a schedule for planned sensory room times each day, depending on the individual's needs.

5. Encourage all senses to be explored and used, but do not force an experience when there is resistance.

6. Continue to be creative in adding activities and ways in which sensory stimuli are introduced.

7. Watch for signs of overstimulation/overarousal/extreme fears and adjust accordingly.

By balancing structure, visual supports and freedom, teachers and parents help their children to develop both their neural organization and the ability to self-regulate.

SUMMARY

Even with prevention and teaching strategies in place, problem behavior will likely occur and require a thoughtful and respectful adult response. The following guidelines help adults to intervene in ways that build positive momentum toward positive behaviors.

• Approach problem behavior as you would a learning error.

• Plan your responses to typical problems in advance.

• Teach students what to do differently.

• Strive for self-regulation and coping strategies.

- Offer solutions that give some control back.

- Consider context and student needs.

- Always build in consequences that teach instead of punish.

- Use strategies that will build positive relationships.

The goal of this book is to help educators and parents to teach young children how to behave. This is not an easy endeavor and will require all the best we have to offer. Along with patience, consistency and dedication, teachers and parents will need to be ready to be flexible and responsive to the immediate needs of the child. While the goal is always prevention of challenging behaviors, every teacher needs to be prepared to intervene once problems do arise, in ways that prevent further escalation and teach a more preferred behavior or coping strategy.

The following final example hopes to illustrate the art and science of building positive momentum toward positive behaviors. After difficulties on the bus and in speech therapy, Bill started to escalate when in the classroom by laughing and twirling and pulling things off the wall. This is a clear indication of increased agitation for this student. The next activity was hygiene and he was offered the choice of doing hygiene or taking a chill pass, given that he was showing signs of escalation toward a bigger problem.

Bill chose a chill pass for ten minutes. After the timer went off, he was directed back to his schedule, but was still not making a positive transition. He was offered the choice again and he chose another ten-minute chill pass. He did this two more times for a total of 35 minutes engaged in the following calming activities:

- building magnets

- counting magnets

- flipping through a book

- decorating a new checklist on the computer.

Bill then transitioned to the hygiene task and completed each of the steps with the support of the teacher and a written checklist.

Bill went on to transition through the rest of the morning schedule successfully from that point forward.

The teacher had a choice to consider at a pivotal moment. She could either keep pushing the original directive of finishing the hygiene task and possibly seeing an escalation of behavior, given the rumbling signs of laughing, twirling, and pulling things off the walls, or offer a chill pass to help the child de-escalate in a positive way in order to regain a sense of calm. By offering the chill pass and honoring the multiple requests, the teacher helped teach that you can manage to prevent your own escalation toward disruptive behaviors with the tools and supports that have been provided and taught. The teacher reflected, at the end of the day, that the 35 minutes spent on what seemed to be non-instructional activities was actually very much instructional. She was teaching Bill how to manage his emotions in positive and proactive ways. This teacher helped him build positive momentum toward positive behaviors. We can do this.

The thought manifests as the word;
The word manifests as the deed;
The deed develops into habit;
And habit hardens into character;
So watch the thought and its ways with care,
And let it spring from love
Born out of concern for all beings...
As the shadow follows the body,
As we think, so we become.

(From the Dhammapada, Sayings of the
Buddha, as cited by Das 1997, p.130)

REFERENCES

Alber, R. (2014) *On-the-Spot Scaffolding for Students.* Edutopia: George Lucas Educational Foundation. Accessed on 28/09/2017 at www.edutopia.org/blog/spot-scaffolding-students-rebecca-alber.

Alter, P.J. and Conroy, M.A. (n.d.) *Preventing Challenging Behavior in Young Children: Effective Practices.* Accessed on 28/09/2017 at www.challengingbehavior.org.

Bellini, S. and Akullian, J. (2007) 'A meta-analysis of video modeling and video self-modeling interventions for children and adolescents with autism spectrum disorders.' (Online version.) *Council for Exceptional Children 73*, 264–287.

Bertone A., Mottron L., Jelenic P. and Faubert J. (2005) Enhanced and diminished visuo-spatial information processing in autism depends on stimulus complexity. *Brain,* October, 128(Pt 10), 2430–2441.

Blair, C. and Diamond, A. (2008) 'Biological processes in prevention and intervention: The promotion of self-regulation as a means of preventing school failure.' *Development and Psychopathology 20*, 899–911.

Bronson, M.B. (2000) *Self-Regulation in Early Childhood: Nature and Nurture.* New York: Guilford.

Bruce, S. (2013) '6 Steps to Conflict Resolution in the Workplace.' *HR Daily Advisor,* 24 June. Accessed on 27/09/2017 at http://hrdailyadvisor.blr.com/2013/06/24/6-steps-to-conflict-resolution-in-the-workplace.

Burdette, H.L. and Whitaker, R.C. (2005) 'Resurrecting free play in young children: Looking beyond fitness and fatness to attention, affiliation, and affect.' *Archives of Pediatrics and Adolescent Medicine 159*, 1, 46–50.

Cohen, E., May-Benson, T., Teasdale, A. and Callahan, M. (2006) *The Relationship Between Behaviors Associated with Sensory Processing and Parents' Sense of Competence.* Watertown, MA: The Spiral Foundation.

Constantino, P.M. and De Lorenzo, M.N. (2001) *Developing a Professional Teaching Portfolio: A Guide for Success.* Boston: Allyn and Bacon.

Crick, N.R., Ostrov, J.M., Burr, J.E., Cullerton-Sen, C., Jansen-Yeh, E. and Ralston, P. (2006) 'A longitudinal study of relational and physical aggression in preschool.' *Journal of Applied Developmental Psychology 27*, 3, 254–268.

Curtis, D. and Carter, M. (2005) 'Rethinking Early Childhood Environments to Enhance Learning.' *Young Children 60*, 3, 34–38.

Das, L.S. (1997) *Eight Steps to Enlightenment: Awakening the Buddha Within: Tibetan Buddhism for the Western World.* New York: Broadway Books.

Dickerson S.S., Gruenewald T.L. and Kemeny M. E. (2004) 'When the social self is threatened: shame, physiology, and health.' *Journal of Personality*, 72, 6, 1191–1216.

Doolittle, J.H. (2006) 'Sustainability of Positive Behavior Supports in Schools.' Unpublished doctoral dissertation, University of Oregon.

Dunlap, G., Strain, P.S., Fox, L. Carta, J.J. *et al.* (2006) 'Prevention and intervention with young children's challenging behavior: Perspectives regarding current knowledge.' *Behavioral Disorders 32*, 1, 29–45.

Dweck, C. (2006) *Mindset*. New York: Ballantine.

Epstein, A.S. (2009) *Me, You, Us: Social-Emotional Learning in Pre-School*. Ypsilanti, MI: HighScope Press.

Epstein, M., Atkins, M., Cullinan, D., Kutash, K. and Weaver, R. (2008) *Reducing Behavior Problems in the Elementary School Classroom: A Practice Guide* (NCEE #2008-012). Washington, DC: National Center for Education Evaluation and Regional Assistance, Institute of Education Sciences, US Department of Education.

Fitzpatrick, M. and Knowlton, E. (2009) 'Bringing evidence-based self-directed intervention practices to the trenches for students with emotional and behavioral disorders.' *Preventing School Failure 53*, 4, 253–266.

Florez, I.R. (2011) *Developing Young Children's Self-Regulation through Everyday Experiences*. Accessed on 25 August 2017 at www.naeyc.org/files/yc/file/201107/Self-Regulation_Florez_OnlineJuly2011.pdf

Fry, D. (2005) 'Rough-and-Tumble Social Play in Humans.' In A.D. Pellegrini and P.K. Smith (eds) *The Nature of Play: Great Apes and Humans* (pp.54–85). New York: Guilford Press.

Galinsky, E. (2010) *Mind in the Making: The Seven Essential Life Skills Every Child Needs*. NAEYC special ed. New York: HarperCollins.

Gartrell, D. (2010) 'Beyond rules to guidelines.' *ChildCare Exchange*, July/August, 52–56.

Gates, B. (2012) 'Shame is not the solution.' *New York Times*, 22 February.

Goleman, D. (1997) *Emotional Intelligence*. New York: Bantam Books.

Gray, C.A. (1994, October) 'Making Sense Out of the World: Social Stories, Comic Strip Conversations, and Related Instructional Techniques.' Paper presented at the Midwest Educational Leadership Conference on Autism, Kansas City, MO.

Hamar, A. (2004) 'Too Loud Lily.' *Children's Book and Media Review 25*, 1, Article 1.

Hemmeter, M.L., Ostrosky, M.M. and Corso, R.M. (2012) 'Preventing and addressing challenging behavior: Common questions and practical strategies.' *Young Exceptional Children 15*, 2, 32–46.

Kaiser, A.P., Hancock, T.B., Cai, X., Foster, E.M. and Hester, P.P. (2000) 'Parent-reported behavioral problems and language delays in boys and girls enrolled in Head Start classrooms.' *Behavioral Disorders 26*, 26–41.

Kelly, A. (1988) 'Gender differences in teacher-pupil interactions: A meta-analytic review.' *Research in Education 39*, 1–23.

Keogh, B.K. (2003) *Temperament in the Classroom: Understanding Individual Differences*. Baltimore, MD: Brookes.

Kerr, M. and Nelson, C. (1989) *Strategies for Managing Behavior Problems in the Classroom* (2nd ed.). New York: Macmillan.

Ladd, G.W. (2008) 'Social competence and peer relations: Significance for young children and their service providers.' *Early Childhood Services 2*, 3, 129-148.

Laguna, S. (2002) *Too Loud Lily*. New York: Scholastic Press.

Lewis, M. and Ramsay, D. (2002) 'Cortisol response to embarrassment and shame.' *Child Development, 73*, 4, 1034-1045.

Maag, J.W. (2000) 'Managing resistance.' *Intervention in School and Clinic 35*, 131-140.

Martens, B.K. and Meller, P.J. (1990) 'The application of behavioral principles to educational settings.' In T.B. Gutkin and C.R. Reynolds (eds) *The Handbook of School Psychology* (2nd ed., pp.612-634). New York: Wiley.

Marzano, R.J., Marzano, J.S. and Pickering, D. (2003) *Classroom Management That Works: Research-Based Strategies for Every Teacher.* Alexandria, VA: Association for Supervision and Curriculum Development.

McCartney, K., Burchinal, M., Clarke-Stewart, A., Bub, K.L., Owen, M.T., Belsky, J. and NICHD Early Child Care Research Network (2010) 'Testing a series of causal propositions relating time in child care to children's externalizing behavior.' *Developmental Psychology 46*, 1, 1-17.

McClowry, S., Rodriguez, E., Tamis-LeMonda, C., Spellman, M., Carlson, A. and Snow, D. (2013) 'Teacher/student interactions and classroom behavior: The role of student temperament and gender.' *Journal of Research in Childhood Education 27*, 283-301.

Miltenberger, R.G. (2008) *Behavior Modification: Principles and Procedures.* Belmont, CA: Thomson Wadsworth.

Newman, L., Davies-Mercier, E. and Marder, C. (2003) 'School Engagement of Youth With Disabilities.' In M. Wagner, C. Marder, J. Blackorby, R. Cameto *et al.* (eds) *The Achievements of Youth With Disabilities During Secondary School.* Menlo Park, CA: SRI International.

Oehler, K. (2013) 'Please don't make me write!' *Autism Asperger's Digest*, January/ February.

Ostrosky, M.M., Jung, E.Y., Hemmeter, M.L. and Thomas, D. (2008) *Helping Children Understand Routines and Classroom Schedules* (What Works Brief Series, No. 3). Champaign, IL: University of Illinois at Urbana-Champaign, Center on the Social and Emotional Foundations for Early Learning.

Pekrun, R., Goetz, T., Perry, R.P., Kramer, K., Hochstadt, M. and Molfenter, S. (2004) 'Beyond test anxiety: Development and validation of the Test Emotions Questionnaire (TEQ).' *Anxiety, Stress, & Coping: An International Journal 17*, 287-316.

Premack, D. (1959) 'Toward empirical behavior laws: 1. Positive reinforcement.' *Psychological Review 66*, 219-233.

Quinn, M.M., Osher, D., Warger, C.L., Hanley, T.V., Bader, B.D. and Hoffman, C.C. (2000) *Teaching and Working with Children Who Have Emotional and Behavioral Challenges.* Longmont, CO: Sopris West.

Readdick, C.A. and Chapman, P.L. (2000) 'Young children's perceptions of time out.' *Journal of Research in Childhood Education 15*, 1, 81-87.

Rudasill, K.M. and Rimm-Kaufman, S.E. (2009) 'Teacher-child relationship quality: The roles of child temperament and teacher-child interactions.' *Early Childhood Research Quarterly 24*, 107-120.

Ryan, R.M. and Deci, E.L. (2016) 'Facilitating and Hindering Motivation, Learning, and Well-Being in Schools: Research and Observations from Self-Determination Theory.' In K.R. Wentzel and D.B. Miele (eds) *Handbook on Motivation at Schools*. New York: Routledge.

Schweinhart, L.J., Montie, J., Xiang, Z., Barnett, W.S., Belfield, C. R., and Nores, M. (2005) *Lifetime Effects: The High/Scope Perry Preschool Study Through Age 40*. Ypsilanti, MI: High/Scope Press.

Sherer, M., Pierce, K.L., Paredes, S., Kisacky, K.L., Ingersoll, B. and Schreibmen L. (2001) 'Enhancing conversation skills in children with autism via video technology: Which is better, "self" or "other" as a model?' *Behavioral Modifications 25*, 1, 140–158.

Snow, K., Thalji, L., Derecho, A., Wheeless, S. *et al.* (2007) *Early Childhood Longitudinal Study, Birth Cohort (ECLS-B), Preschool Data File User's Manual (2005–06)* (NCES 2007-055). US Department of Education. Washington, DC: National Center for Education Statistics.

Sousa, D. (2006) *How the Brain Learns* (3rd ed.). Thousand Oaks, CA: Corwin.

Stage, S.A. and Quiroz, D.R. (1997) 'A meta-analysis of interventions to decrease disruptive classroom behavior in public education settings.' *School Psychology Review 26*, 3, 333–368.

Stormont, M., Lewis, T.J. and Covington Smith, S. (2005) 'Behavior support strategies in early childhood settings: Teachers' importance and feasibility ratings.' *Journal of Positive Behavior Interventions 7*, 3, 131–139.

Tangney, J.P. and Dearing, R. (2002) *Shame and Guilt in Interpersonal Relationships*. New York: Guilford Press.

Thompson, R. (2001) 'The roots of school readiness in social and emotional development.' *The Kauffman Early Education Exchange 1*, 8–29.

Tremblay R.E., Daniel S., Nagin J., Seguin R. et al. (2004) Physical aggression during early childhood: Trajectories and predictors. *Pediatrics, 114*, e43–e50.

University of California–Berkeley (2014) *How Chronic Stress Predisposes Brain to Mental Disorders*. ScienceDaily, 11 February. Accessed on 28/09/17 at www.sciencedaily.com/releases/2014/02/140211153559.htm.

US Department of Education (2010) *Thirty-Five Years of Progress in Educating Children With Disabilities Through IDEA*. Accessed on 28/09/2017 at www2.ed.gov/about/offices/list/osers/idea35/history/idea-35-history.pdf.

Webster-Stratton, C. and Taylor, T. (2001) 'Nipping early risk factors in the bud: Preventing substance abuse, delinquency, and violence in adolescence through interventions targeted at young children (0–8 years).' *Prevention Science 2*, 165–192.

Wong, H.K. and Wong, R.T. (1998) *The First Days of School: How to Be an Effective Teacher*. Mountain View, CA: Harry K. Wong Publications.

INDEX